On Wildlife Denver

TRUE NORTH

Reflections on Fishing and a Life Well Lived

JACK KULPA

THE DERRYDALE PRESS
Lanham and New York

THE DERRYDALE PRESS

Published in the United States of America by
The Derrydale Press
A Member of the Rowman & Littlefield Publishing Group
4720 Boston Way, Lanham, Maryland 20706

Distributed by NATIONAL BOOK NETWORK, INC.

Library of Congress Control Number: 2002110056

ISBN 1-58667-081-6 (cl.: alk. paper)

♾ ™ The paper used in this publication meets the minimum requirements
of American National Standard for Information Sciences—Permanence of
Paper for Printed Library Materials, ANSI/NISO Z39.48-1992.
Manufactured in the United States of America.

This book is for
Peggy
and
Nicholas

Contents

Part Two: Summer

Part Three: Autumn

Part Four: Winter

Acknowledgments

Much of the material in this book appeared—sometimes slightly altered, and occasionally under different titles—in the following magazines:

Field & Stream: "True North," "The Old Silences," "Pike Magic," "The Rune of Loons," "Reefer Creek," "Stormbound," "The Gloaming," "Portage Trails," "Little Victories," "Fare Game," "Summer Dreams," "In Praise of Perch," "Brigadoon," "Red Camp," "Paths of Enlightenment," "Alone in the Woods," "Second Chances"

Sports Afield: "Waiting for Spring," "The Ledge," "The Land That Time Forgot," "Castle Creek," "The Wind in the Wire," "The Wishing Well"

Fur-Fish-Game: "Lost Lake," "The Lonesome"

Wisconsin Outdoor Journal: "Spring Cleaning"

"Pine Knots: Survivors from Our Ancient Forests" is reprinted here by permission of *Wisconsin Sportsman*.

"Far Horizons" appeared under the title "A Solo Adventure" and was originally published by *Wisconsin Trails* magazine.

Portions of "Abbey Lake" originally appeared under the title "Jack-Pine Bass" and is reprinted by permission from the June 2000 issue of *Bassmaster Magazine*, Montgomery, Ala.

Writers, like fishermen, exaggerate. For all the blather about writing being a solitary profession, the truth is no writer was ever published without the help of editors. In my own case, I am deeply indebted to:

Slaton L. White and Mike Toth of *Field & Stream*, for extending me unbounded kindness, consideration, and opportunity.

Tom Paugh and Fred Kesting. During their tenure at *Sports Afield*, they were the first to present my fish tales to a national audience.

Vin T. Sparano and Merritt Benson. While at *Outdoor Life*, they gave me my first assignment as an outdoor writer and provided me with encouragement when I most needed it.

To Peter Burford, who brought my work to the attention of The Derrydale Press.

To Stephen Driver and The Derrydale Press, who made this book possible.

And to Francis de Sales, the patron saint of writers.

Foreword
True North

"I have laid aside business, and gone a-fishing."

—Izaak Walton
The Compleat Angler

When I was a kid in the 1950s, heading "Up North" was a summer ritual. This was in the days when my father drove a Packard and *The Shadow* could still cloud men's minds on the radio.

In June, after school let out, Dad would cram half his house, most of his family, and all his fishing gear into the Packard, and then point the automobile toward Wisconsin's Northwoods. We lived in Milwaukee, but the ritual was the same in Minneapolis, Chicago, or Detroit. Tell any Midwesterner that you were "headin' Up North," and they would know exactly what you were doing.

"Going fishing, eh?" they'd ask.

In those days before Alaska became a state, northern Wisconsin had the best fishing in America. Eisenhower was president at the time, and Wisconsin was where he went to catch fish. Before Ike, Herbert Hoover came here to cast a line, and Calvin Coolidge once spent an entire summer fishing the Brule River while running the country from a makeshift White House set up at a high school in the town of Superior. Even now, Wisconsin sells more non-resident fishing licenses than any other state, and if the fishing isn't what it used to be, it's still better than most places I've visited. With over 15,000 lakes, 9,500 miles of trout streams, and 600 miles of shoreline on the Great Lakes, it's tough not to catch fish in Wisconsin.

Like most Wisconsinites, my father had a predilection for walleyes, and our usual destination in the 1950s was Glassy Lake. The blacktop ended twenty miles from the lake, in a town that called itself "The Walleye Capital." The town had wooden sidewalks, and along both sides of Main Street stood freezer cases with glass lids. Under the glass were dozens of fat, hefty walleyes caught by vacationing fishermen. There were mounted walleyes in the bait shops, taverns, gas stations, grocery store, and post office. The town even had a Walleye Queen—she once served me an ice cream cone at the Tastee-Freeze. It's the closest I've come to hobnobbing with royalty.

We always stopped at the Swede's bait shop. The Swede kept a fleet of leaky, wooden rowboats cached among the backcountry lakes, and for $5 the boat at Glassy Lake was ours for the week.

Dad always asked if the walleyes were biting.

"You bat you!" the Swede would say.

"The fishing's good?" Dad would ask.

"Ya. Iss goot. You bat you."

Later I'd ask Dad if he understood the Swede.

"You bat you!" Dad would say. It was our private joke for forty years.

*   *   *

These are the waking reveries of a middle-aged man. I pour another cup of coffee, trying to flood my sleep-addled senses with caffeine-induced clarity. Outside the cabin's window, rosy ribbons fill the eastern sky, harbingers of another day or new adventure—I'm free to choose. The dark spires of spruce trees rise like steeples against the lightening sky; the lonely whistle of a white-throated sparrow is the morning's matins. Down at the lake a bass jumps in the shallows; the resultant ripples sweep away the shadows from the flawless tarn. I check the reel and rod again, tie a popper to my line, adjust the strap on my waders, and step outside. Thoreau wrote: "If I should sell both my forenoons and afternoons to society, there would be nothing left worth living for." I trade most of my forenoons and afternoons to society, but this day is mine. This day I'm going fishing.

*   *   *

Nowadays I live in the Lake Superior country of northwestern Wisconsin, not far from the headwaters of the St. Croix—one of the original streams designated as a wild river by the Wild And Scenic Rivers Act of 1968. The cabin I've built here sits between the St. Croix and Namekagon, and nearby lie the Clam, Yellow, Moose, Eau Claire, and Totagatic Rivers. In addition to the rivers and countless creeks, a thousand lakes encircle my cabin, each piece of water more lovely and secluded than the last. This is one of only four areas in the world where there is nearly as much water as land. Tourist bureaus refer to this region as Wisconsin's "Fish Bowl." I call it home.

My cabin sits near the end of a narrow dirt road beside tiny Lucerne Lake. Just big enough for one or two friends and whatever gear we need for fishing, I built it as a getaway. Lately, I've been getting away a lot. Unlike others who go to the woods to "rough it," I come here to smooth life's imperfect edges and to take Socrates' advice to heart: "The life which is unexamined is not worth living." Fishing is the lens through which I look; lakes and streams provide the reflections. And what I find—more often than not—are mysteries, wonder, riddles, and runes.

*   *   *

Looking back, I realize that mystery had much to do with the summer trips my Dad made in search of walleyes. Back then, walleye fishing was something you did at night or before dawn. At the first glimpse of sunlight, the walleyes vanished as if struck by a wizard's wand. The fish might bite like lunatics until pink streamers filled the eastern sky. Then, suddenly and inexplicably, the walleyes were gone.

It was spooky. For one thing, no one really knew where the walleyes went when they disappeared. We only knew it was someplace deep and unfathomable. During the day I'd fish for perch, but I was always peering into the dark-jeweled water, trying to find the walleyes' secret world.

It wasn't until the owls began to hoot that the walleyes reappeared. At the first hint of dusk, Dad would take the white gas lantern down to the lakeshore, and load the boat with our gear. Back then, walleye tackle was primitive: it consisted of one-piece

Namekagon and the season was open, I'd be tossing spinners until I caught the fish or dropped dead. But halfway to McDowell's Bridge the new ache in my right shoulder told me I'd had enough. Early arthritis, a doctor had said. I put aside the rod and paddle, and let the canoe drift downstream.

My wife, Peg, was waiting at McDowell's with the pickup. She asked about the trip, the fishing, and if I wanted an aspirin for my shoulder. I said I'd take the aspirin, and when we got back to the cabin I'd take a little Black Bush, too. For the pain.

Fifty is not old, but it is a long time to live without real tragedy striking close to home. Anyone who makes it to fifty with only a little arthritis to remind him of his age is luckier than many, or perhaps most. On the ride back to the cabin, I began thinking about things I'd like to do before I was too old to do them. A few items from my usual wish list came to mind: hike across Europe with a knapsack and pack rod; fish away a summer in The Valley of Ten Thousand Smokes; canoe from Lake Superior to Hudson Bay. The problem was that I would have to sacrifice real dreams to finance these excursions; and these trips were, for the most part, not dreams but fantasies. There is a difference.

That night I walked down in the dusk to Lucerne Lake, feeling a little melancholy about turning fifty, and painfully aware of the passing of time. I had come down to the dock to simply sit and think, but all around me largemouths were slurping up the last hatch of mayflies and I admonished myself for having left the rod up at the cabin. All life is transilient. Only the fishing is not.

*   *   *

Now that I'm thoroughly middle-aged, I know that walleyes are not terrific battlers, but as a kid—fishing in the dark with Dad steel rods, backlashing baitcasting reels, a box of sinkers hooks, and a galvanized bucket of shiner minnows.

The boat's rusty oarlocks would wobble and clunk as rowed us into the gathering dark. Shorelines teemed with light and silence, and in the hush I could hear big fish ju near shore.

"Let's try over there," I'd say, pointing to where a fi just broken the lake's unruffled surface.

"Those are bass," Dad would say. "We're after walley

We knew nothing of depthfinders or hydrographic n stead, Dad would "read" shorelines to locate submerge and drop-offs. We'd row upwind of those places, bait o drop them over the side, and drift.

We huddled in the lantern's light with darkness p from every side, watching our rod tips for the "tap" t signal a strike. We were fishing for walleyes but never to expect, other than the simple fascination of watc slice through black water. And then, without warning would quiver.

"Got one!" I'd cry, as Dad grabbed the net.

*   *   *

Last weekend I turned fifty. I celebrated my bi ing for smallmouths on the Namekagon. I put my the Burnett-Washburn county line, floating the McDowell's Bridge. I could see their shadows water before I'd cast to them, the bronzebacks s ner as only smallmouths can, bursting like firecr they jumped free of the surface. Ordinarily I'm a comes to fishing—if there was only one smallm on Glassy Lake—every walleye fought like a wolf. The things had teeth; and then there were those incredible eyes—blank, luminous, inscrutable, haunting.

Walleyes seemed to shun my world. Unlike the bass, pike, and panfish that I saw in the sunny shallows during the day, walleyes preferred the night and lambent depths of an icy, unplumbed lake. Theirs was a world so distant and different from my own that I was sure it was a place only walleyes knew about— a place more remote and mysterious than the moon.

"Look at those stars!" Dad would say. "Can you find Polaris?"

And I'd find it easily at the end of the Little Dipper, hovering brightly, as it still does, above True North.

That was forty years ago. Since then, things have grown complex. Instead of just fishing, I'm often caught up in spoonplugging, back-trolling, or downrigging—and I haven't seen a leaky, wooden rowboat in years. I no longer need to read shorelines; computer graphics do it better. And Dad wouldn't begin to understand limnology. Nor would he understand the anxiety and confusion of life in the Twenty-First century.

Yet for all that, the basics of fishing remain unchanged. Oh, I toss the latest crankbaits and plugs into all the right places, but I'm also content to drop a baited hook over the side of the boat and hope the fish are there. In terms of technique, it's as primitive as a Packard. But as a means of anchoring myself in this inconstant world, it's as steadfast as Polaris, pointing to True North.

PART ONE

SPRING

ONE

Waiting for Spring

Only those who have spent a winter in the North can understand the importance of opening day on Lake Superior's steelhead streams. Only those who have watched the snow climb to the eaves of a cabin roof, waited while the mercury lay below zero for endless weeks, and wondered if the woodpile out in the yard would last another month, can know the thrill of working the first ice-rimmed pool of open water. To experience it you must wait for it, longing for its arrival with the same urgency of a trout struggling upstream to spawn. For in a land where lakes and rivers are bound in ice for half the year, the steelhead opener is more than the start of just another fishing season—it is the light at the end of winter's long gauntlet.

I had been waiting a long time. For weeks I had been checking and preparing my gear, sharpening hooks and patching waders. Each night I went down to the river to check on how much ice had gone out and to reassure myself that the open stretches of water would remain open. I was like a boy preparing for summer camp six weeks in advance.

When the day arrived I jumped out of bed long before sunrise, rushing about the cabin like a man late for a date. Breakfast was a cup of coffee and a muffin smothered in wild rose petal jam—spring was dawning and there was no time to lose. Then I was out the door, out into the woods, ready to begin the first and most important foray of the season.

Much of the river was shrouded in ice, and the snow lay knee-deep along its banks. Only the week before I had come across a deer yard in the Flag River country, a few miles east, where the conifers and young aspen had been stripped bare of browse and bark to a height of eight feet. The dried and frozen carcasses of deer littered the earth like autumn leaves. South of the Lake Superior country, where winters are more mild and Wisconsin hunters harvest more than 300,000 whitetails each year, the horror of a March deer yard is unknown. But in the North, where only a few deer are taken by a relative handful of hunters or an occasional timber wolf, only the strong survive the wait for spring. All others die the long death of hunger.

Now, in the balsam thicket ahead of me, a deer snorted, and when I looked up I saw the bright flags of three big animals bounding away through the brush. It was a good sign. The yards were breaking up and the deer were once again moving freely through the woods. Ten minutes later, at the first pool, I jumped a flock of black ducks. They bolted for the sky while an otter on the far bank made a headlong rush for the stream. Suddenly life was all around me, and for the first time in months I felt that my own hunger for spring would soon be satisfied.

The banks along the river were thick with balsams, and the air was filled with their sharp, sweet perfume. I crushed a few needles in the palm of my hand, and when I held them to my nose, the fragrance of balsam resin nearly made me swoon. It was the scent of the North, of campsites and forest glens, and of bedrolls laid out beneath the light of blazing stars. It made me think of wilderness lakes and whitewater rivers, and all the many things I associated with the Lake Superior woods. It would be several weeks before portage trails were fit for travel, and almost as long before rivers were safe to run. But things were changing quickly and I was filled with an old and familiar excitement, brimming with anticipation of things to come.

I tied a bit of blaze orange yarn to the shank of a steelhead hook, threaded a single pink salmon egg over the shaft and barb, and tossed the whole works into the current. The high water was the cloudy color of coffee with cream, and before I could shut the reel's bail, the rage of the swollen river carried the bait far downstream.

Where I could, I worked the river slowly, letting the bait drift into the riffles at the edges of pools; letting the stream carry it beneath undercut banks submerged in flood; watching as it moved past old snags, around rocks and through deep holes; always ready, always watching, always waiting for that first strike.

I fished deliberately, wanting to make each cast count, wanting the feeling and awareness of being on open water again to last as long as it could. I worked most slowly and carefully in the long, narrow stretch of flat water known as The Meadows. It was the finest place on the river to fish, and the biggest trout were always taken there each season. In two or three weeks, steelhead would jam those narrows like a run of salmon. But now, on opening day, only ice floes filled the stream.

Near the Lenroot Ledges I came across a group of anglers who had come up from the South for the fishing. I could hear it in the way they complained about the wintry weather and poor fishing, and I could see it, too, in the way they rushed from hole to hole, as if the thing they sought might be waiting for them at the next pool, the next eddy, the next bend. I searched their eyes for signs of spring, but all I found was their quiet fear that they might run out of time before running out of river. I recognized the look: I had seen it in my own eyes during the longest nights of winter, when all I could think about was the return of spring. It was one of the scars garnered in wanting a thing too much—a trophy fish, a better job, a truer love, a different life.

Another time I came across a solitary angler working a lonely pool with the same sincere and careful concentration I had used, so immersed in the moment that I passed unnoticed in the brush. Later I found another fisherman sitting alone on a spit of rock at Lower Falls, pole out of the water and hip boots peeled down to the knees, basking in an April sun whose zenith barely rose above the trees.

"Any luck?" I asked.

"Luck?" The old man looked genuinely shocked at the question. Then he smiled, wide as the river. "Hell, I feel lucky just to be sittin' here on a day like this." He spit a stream of to-bacco juice into the slush of the river, then grinned at me from beneath the bill of his cap. "I can't say much for the fishin', though," he said.

He was an old-timer who had a shack on one of the tote roads near Reefer Creek, and, like me, he had wintered over in the woods. Like me, he too had been drawn to the river by the spell of opening day. For us and for others like us, the fishing was only an excuse.

*   *   *

When Wisconsin's Lake Superior steelhead season opens on or about April Fool's Day each year, a thousand anglers may converge on the Bois Brule, the bluest of the Midwest's blue-ribbon trout streams. Surprisingly, most of them know that not one man in fifty will net a fish that day. The big fish that entered the Brule in autumn and wintered over in the river are far upstream of where fishing is allowed; the second run of spawning steelhead will not leave Lake Superior in any real numbers until almost May, when the rivers shed the last of their ice. Still, like the trout they seek, the same people return to the same streams on opening day.

I have some theories about that. Perhaps the observance of opening day satisfies some deep and primitive need in us for signs and portents. Perhaps it touches some deep and unplumbed recess of the subconscious, recalling a time long ago when mists and magic ruled the earth, and men greeted spring's return with joy and holy ritual. In those days the equinox was the harbinger of spring, and those who survived the winter were assured of a life in the coming season. But nowadays, in a world where life can be manufactured in a petri dish and survival is a balanced checkbook, the miracle of spring's renaissance seems wanting.

Yet anyone who has wintered over in the North and endured the long watch for spring's portents knows that the hunger and the need to be on a stream come opening day is as real as the ancients' longing for equinox. Whether or not the trout are there is of no consequence. What matters is the act of fishing, of simply being there, alive and well and aware. For although the mysteries of existence have been dispelled, life remains a fleeting thing, soon spent and easily lost.

*   *   *

Just before dark I went down to the river's mouth. I was alone there, and before me lay the wide, frozen expanse of Lake Superior, as stark and cruel as a polar landscape. It would be

another month before the last snowstorm swept down from the
Canadian side of the lake, and I would have to wait until June for
the first leaves of balsam poplar to unfurl before the bleak, winter woods were once again green and alive and lush. But the deer
were free of the tombs of their yards, the black ducks had returned, and otters were once again sunning along streambanks.
It was only a glimpse of spring—a harbinger, an omen, a sign of
things to come—but for now it was enough. I had crossed the
hump.

When the sun set, the temperature dropped twenty degrees
and my mustache turned stiff and brittle with ice. The wind
shifted, swinging around to the northeast, coming in off the wide
and barren lake with nothing to break it but the endless, empty
miles of frozen space. I turned my back to it, but even my wool
coat could not stop the goosebumps. Sharp, stinging snow began
to blow. Out on the lake the ice boomed and cracked with the
freeze. The water on my monofilament solidified into hard beads
of translucent crystal.

I dipped my rod in the river to free the line guides of slush
and made another cast. I followed it with another, then another,
and still another, until my hands began to sting and throb, forcing me to pull on my wool-lined leather mittens.

It was winter again, and it would remain winter, off and on,
for a few more weeks, until one day the last of the snow would be
gone from the north slope of the cabin's roof and robins would
again sing in the pines outside the windows.

A great gray owl began to call among the spruces across the
stream, and I reeled in my ice-clogged line and broke apart my
gear, heading up the hill away from the river. I was going home
without a fish, but it didn't matter.

There are some things that cannot be made to happen, some things that cannot be made subject to the will. Wishing for both springtime and good fishing along the banks of a northern river this time of year are just two of many such things. The best anyone can do is to go there, believing, and wait for it to happen. Sooner or later what you seek will come. And while you wait, you have stolen a little time from all the days and hours of a life that too often speed by like the torrent of a thaw-swollen stream. Soon enough the fair weather passes, and all that remains is the waiting for spring.

TWO

The Old Silences

Once a year, for a few short days in April, the old silences return to the North. It happens in the wake of warm winds and sunny days, when the deep snows of winter begin to vanish. Rivers are in flood, dirt roads are mires, and blue skies call with the clamor of passing geese. Now, for a little while, the wilderness lies abandoned, as alone and isolated as it used to be.

The old silences are something more than mere quiet and calm. They are the timeless silences of wild places, far from the press of cares and crowds. They are the subtle rhythms of earth in motion, and the natural cycles that shape and give it life. Sound is a part of it: the rushing winds of early April, the swelling roar of thawing streams, the distant high calling of migrating birds, and the first cadences of spring. But solitude is a part of it too, for without solitude silence is lost.

I caught a hint of the old silences one morning along the Brule River. It was April, but where the stream enters Lake Superior the rotting snow lay half as tall as a man. The wind was up, jostling white birches, but with a gentleness akin to a whisper. After long months of relentless cold and snow and icy

Below the ledge I spotted a big fish lying near the surface beside a bank of flooded alders, its broad back barely visible in the cloudy stream. In the noon sunlight more fish would expose themselves in this way, seeking the comfort of shallow and slightly warmer water. I tied a length of yarn to a short-shanked hook buried in a salmon egg. After a dozen casts the torpid fish took the bait, but so lightly that I missed the telltale tap and ended up snagging the alders. I watched the fish—a big steelhead—swim away.

Later I walked the bank in the fresh tracks of a bear, following the trail back to a haystack of windfalls. The bear had denned there for a time, but now, like me, it was scouting the river for signs of spring. Soon it would leave the stream for more secluded reaches, and by the time May's fair-weather fishermen arrived all that would remain would be a few washed-out tracks. But for now the river belonged to the bear again, as rivers always do when silence and solitude are unbroken.

Late that afternoon I took another brown. Like the big steelhead I had seen, my fish had been lying near the surface at the bank. I made several casts upstream of the fish, following with my rod tip as the bait drifted with the river. I held the line in front of the reel between a finger and thumb, feeling the bait bounce in the current until it suddenly stopped. In the brutally cold water the trout were lethargic, and when the fish struck it felt like a pause in the drift. Then came the tap against the taut line's resistance. I pulled back on the rod and set the hook.

The brown went better than a pound; its flanks gleamed like precious metal. Fresh from the icy water, its flesh was firm and as pink as a salmon's. I plucked wintercress from along the stream and wrapped the fish in the leaves, and then wrapped it again in a sheet of aluminum foil from my pack. I built a small fire and boiled water for tea, and then placed the fish on the glowing embers. There may be sweeter delicacies than Darjeeling tea brewed from snowmelt and freshly caught trout cooked in wintercress, but none can compare when savored in solitude beside an open fire. And though there would be other feasts and campfires in the days ahead, none would mean as much as this—the first of the season.

It was dusk when I left the river, and with the twilight came a deepening hush. Silence filled the river's chasm until it was brimming with the absence of sound. Gone now was the calling of killdeer and finches, the rushing wind, the rumbling stream. Fog and moonlight flooded the river, accentuating the calm and peace.

Soon I'd be sharing the river with others, and when that time came the silence would be less profound, but for now evening mists were swirling soundlessly along the river, while the pike continued their ageless journey toward ancestral spawning grounds. The black bear would be prowling his woods in solitude, unseen, unheard, and undisturbed, and at Indian Rock ghosts would be gathering in the moonlight, as they always do when the old silences return.

THREE

Pike Magic

In the Lake Superior country, the spring spawning run of pike has a special significance. Here, where life and lakes are inanimate from November to May, the migration of northern pike is an event that those of us who live in the North dream about for half the year.

There's no knowing when the run will happen. In some years, pike may even make their runs under the ice. More often, it occurs after the first thaw. When woods fill with the steady trickle of snowmelt and rivers brim with floodwater, pike are already migrating upstream to ancient spawning grounds.

This year it happened toward the end of April. Winter was all but gone from the woods: the snow lay only in patches or on the north sides of hills. In the wake of the thaw even tiny streams roared like torrents: overnight, frozen lakes were rent by blue leads of open water. Then, one morning I awoke in the dark and heard the trilling of the first robin, the surest sign that spring had returned.

Breakfast was a quick cup of coffee. I was sure the pike had started to move and I wanted to be there to see it happen. The open season on pike was still weeks away, but now was the time to find where the pike were running. Balsam Creek topped my list of places to check. I know Balsam Creek, though I don't know it well. It is one of those many remote and often nameless streams that create the rivers that feed the Great Lakes. These little streams exist wherever the headwaters of inland lakes and rivers occur. A few are fished by trout enthusiasts, but most go unvisited for years. Yet in early spring, when these creeks flood with snowmelt, they are also apt to be swollen with northern pike. It's then that pike run in these creeks to deposit eggs far upstream in the sheltered and relatively warm water of flooded marshes.

Two sorts of pike turn up in these places in spring: native fish that remain within the watershed throughout the year and pike that migrate from Lake Superior to spawn far inland. The native fish are dark and mossy, with orange-tinged fins. Lake-run pike are pale pewter, flecked with ivory and gold, and both fatter and longer; but should receding water levels, a shifting sandbar, or other obstacle trap them within the watershed, they will turn as dark as the native pike.

Both kinds of pike can be caught with fly-fishing, spin-casting, or bait-casting gear, but most are probably taken on spinning gear. This is especially true on large streams where a 6-1/2-foot medium action spinning rod lets you make the long casts that are required to sweep bait down wide stretches of water. On small creeks, a long spinning rod can guide the bait in and around obstructions, down into feeding lanes, and into likely looking places below undercut banks.

Eight-pound monofilament is the best all-around line for pike fishing, especially when casting with live bait or light lures. Its relatively small diameter drags less than heavier lines and holds up well to rocks and other abrasions; it also drifts bait naturally after long casts. All this is important when fishing streams. It's also prudent to use a wire leader—a pike's toothy mouth will cut through even the thickest nylon stringer.

*   *   *

I followed an old logging trail through spruces and birches, paralleling a river that was only a black gash of rushing water between high banks still white with snow. In places the snow on the trail was still knee-deep, but the crust was hard enough to walk on and would stay that way until the sun rose above the trees at noon.

The trail ended where Balsam Creek joined the river. I stood there a moment, listening to the tumult of the thaw-swollen water, the wind in the trees, and the trilling of robins among the naked alders. Then I turned upstream along Balsam Creek. The banks were already sunny with hepatica, the first flower of spring. The land grew steep and in places the creek roared through rocks or tumbled over ledges and logjams.

Suddenly and without warning, I saw a fish as long as my arm jump upstream, hurdling a rock ledge. Almost instantly another pike leapt into the air behind it. I bulldozed my way through the alders to the edge of the stream and saw other fish in the pool below the ledge.

Perhaps a score of pike were holding themselves steady against the current below the ledge. Then, as if on cue, they began to move as one, throwing themselves up and over the ledge, propelled by a relentless urge to move upstream. I watched as pike of all sizes hurled themselves at the ledge. The strongest and biggest fish leapt clear of it on their first attempt; many others fell short of the mark and crashed against the rocks before being swept downstream. Yet in a moment they were back to try again.

The pool foamed white with turbulence as the fish lunged at the rocks. And then, as suddenly as they had appeared, the pike vanished. But this was only passing. I knew other fish would soon appear to take the place of those I had seen.

*   *   *

Two weeks later, when the season opened, I was startled at how far the Balsam had receded; it was almost narrow enough to jump. In another two weeks it would be only a trickle. Most of the fish had long since deposited their eggs upstream and returned to the river below, but I was sure there would be stragglers in the Balsam's pools.

The creek had developed holes immediately downstream of its rapids and ledges, and below logs and other flotsam that created natural dams. Pike were likely to be anyplace where the water had had a chance to scour a depression into the creekbed. There the fish would remain until low water and warm days pulled them back to the river.

My gear was simple: a medium-action spinning rod, 8-pound line, and a slim wire leader with a wide-bend hook. From my shoulder hung a canvas creel filled with frozen smelt.

It's hard to think of a better bait for northerns than smelt. Pike favor the oily little fish more than they do suckers and chubs, and they will readily attack dead smelt—which makes packing bait into remote places a lot easier.

I had netted smelt only the week before, during the peak of their run. In April they come out of the depths of the Great Lakes and run along shorelines in vast schools before entering rivers to spawn. On a good night, two men with a seine or long-handled dip nets can fill a washtub with the silvery fish. After cleaning and freezing enough smelt for my own table, I freeze several dozen smaller packages of smelt to use as pike bait throughout the year. For the angler who doesn't have access to smelt or otherwise shuns live bait, bucktail spinners and tandem spinnerbaits will catch spawn-driven northerns.

I slipped my hook below a 6-inch smelt's back fin and clipped enough split shot above the leader to keep the bait moving along the creekbottom. I made a cast to the head of the pool where I'd seen pike leap just days before, dropping the bait in front of the ledge and letting the current carry it downstream.

In spring, when water is icy, drift-fishing for pike is a lot like casting for steelhead. Keeping the rod tip high telegraphs what the bait is doing, as does keeping a taut line and holding it between thumb and finger. Later, when leaves unfurl and temperatures soar, pike will pounce on dead smelt. But until then a strike from a northern pike will simply feel like a pause in the drift.

I almost missed the first strike. I felt the split shot stop bouncing along the creekbottom—and then my line sliced through the water as the pike picked up the smelt and moved upstream. I forced myself to wait and not set the hook until the fish swallowed the bait.

Pike are notorious for mouthing bait and carrying it away without getting hooked, especially in frigid water—as anyone who has fished for pike through the ice can attest. Pike usually strike live bait and then swim with it for some distance before stopping to turn the bait lengthwise in their mouths in order to swallow. Pull back on your rod too soon and you'll yank the bait from the pike's mouth. Wait too long and your line may get hopelessly tangled around some underwater obstruction.

In spring, I set the hook as if I were ice-fishing: I counted to twenty, reeled in the slack line, and pulled up and back on the rod. When the fish came up and thrashed at the surface it looked as big as a fence post. Later, when I placed the tape against it, the fish went 30-inches and was half that again in girth.

Horizontal flecks of ivory speckled the pike's flanks; under them, the fish was viridescent with shades of silver and gold. The pale, bright colors marked it as a lake-run pike fresh from Lake Superior; it had likely been in the stream for only a few days. I laid the fish on a smooth log and slit its underside. A 10-inch ribbon of spawn fell from its belly. I cut the fish into steaks and placed these in the canvas creel.

I moved upstream and took two more pike below a logjam. Like the first, they were lake-run fish, heavy and laden with spawn. The logjam was the final barrier to the pike's spawning grounds, and in the pool below it a dozen pike slithered and squirmed. These I saved for another day; to me, they were like money in the bank—an investment for my future, or perhaps another's.

Above the logjam lay a flooded swale studded with the silver stubs of tamarack. Tufts of yellow marsh grass were clearly visible above the water. In the high grass, spring peepers made a sound like jingling bells. It was here, in water that barely reached the tops of my boots, that the pike came to spawn.

Water had already receded from much of the meadow, leaving millions of eggs to rot in the grass. Many more eggs would be lost when the stream fell back within its banks. And yet, miraculously, some would survive to become the latest link in a chain as old as life itself.

I looked down and saw a pike wiggling through the flooded grass, its back barely covered by the shallow water. Then my eyes grew accustomed to the weedy, tea-stained water, and I saw another fish slithering through the flooded tussocks.

Spring had returned and while it lasted Balsam Creek would teem with pike—along with the mystery of migration, and the wonder that is life.

FOUR

The Ledge

Wisconsin's White River is a young man's river. Below the old lumbering town of Mason, the White drops sharply in its plunge toward Lake Superior, creating a twelve-mile stretch of continuous rapids before reaching the dam near Sanborn. Any canoeist who makes that run commits himself to the river, for along that stretch steep clay cliffs rise like ramparts from the water, difficult to descend and impossible to climb. The tops of the bluffs are battlements of solid timber, and beyond them lies a roadless wilderness of balsam, spruce, and pine. A man is on his own if he finds trouble in that chasm, and in early spring trouble can lurk at every bend. Indians say only young fools run rapids—but in spring, the White belongs to reckless young men.

I was thinking about that as I stood on the bridge outside Mason. The White was high and cloudy with snowmelt, and the bare woods of early May were filled with its roar. Below me, at the canoe landing, red-winged blackbirds called from dry cattails, the sere stalks submerged in a foot of slush. I watched as a popple log came racing down the river and vanished in the torrents below the first drop.

Each year, for some time now, I had run the White in spring. The White is one of the finest trout streams in Wisconsin, but even the most avid anglers avoid the twelve-mile stretch of quick-water between Mason and the dam. One reason is the lack of access: no roads or bridges cross the flume, and the old logging trails that once led there have been obliterated by brush. The only practical way to fish it is to run its rapids, but a practical person would never risk the run. As a result, there are long stretches of the White that no one ever fishes.

Because of this, I thought of the White as being *my* river: in all my visits, I never once met another man along its banks. Of course, no one can *own* a river, but anyone who reached the White was free to think of it as his. I had risked its rapids and fished its secret places; consequently, I thought of the White as a personal possession.

Now, standing on the bridge and looking down into the rushing water, I reconsidered my plan to run the White yet another time. After all, I was getting older—old enough to know that a spill in the icy water would mean an ordeal. But then I thought about the river's unspoiled fishing, the chance to spend time alone in a wild and beautiful place, and that intangible quality that has to do with quickwater and quick wits and the good feeling that comes after doing a thing no one else would dare to do. I looked down into the river and knew it would be waiting for me somewhere downstream among the rapids—that sudden, shining, fleeting moment when I always felt most keenly that I was alive.

I secured my gear in the canoe. Ten miles downstream lay "The Rock," a sandstone ledge that jutted out from the root of a palisade bluff, forming a long, slick pool of flatwater. In early spring, after the ice was out but before the woods were green, The Rock held some of the river's finest fishing. It was then that big brown trout prowled the pool, striking from the submerged recesses of the ledge. The fishing alone was worth the risk of running the White in flood.

As soon as I pushed off I felt the grip of the current and knew there could be no turning back. The swollen stream was unpredictable and swift, and I was instantly swept up in its spumes and swirls and rocks. Occasionally there was a short stretch of flatwater, with time enough to catch a breath. But then the river plunged again in its race for Lake Superior, and all my concentration was on watching for breaks between the rocks.

The last rapids before The Rock are the most harrowing: a five-foot tumble down a narrow chute that drops quickly, as a falls. I came through it and hit the backroller waiting at the bottom, and the impact was like running head-on into a wall. I could feel the turbulence wanting to suck the canoe down from under me, and the only way out of the vortex was to risk a spill by leaning far downstream while reaching for the moving current with the paddle. I dug in, deep, and the bow spun around, and then the canoe seemed to fly as it hurdled the wall of standing water. In a moment it was over—the pitch was passed—and then came the thrill of looking back and seeing what only a fool would try to beat. I drifted with the current toward the start of The Rock, cold, wet, and shivering with excitement.

Then I saw him—and when I did, all the joy went out of me.

He was standing on The Rock, at the lip of the ledge, looking upstream at me. My first reaction was surprise and then annoyance at the thought of having to share The Rock with another angler. It wasn't until I ran the canoe up into the landing place that the intruder moved. He walked toward me, slow as if in a dream, and as he came closer I saw that he was very old.

He was tiny, stoop-shouldered and listing to one side, his furrowed face as tan as a biscuit. He walked in a slow, arthritic shuffle, as though each step were a painful event. Seeing that, my resentment waned a little. Obviously the old fool had walked to the river, and I couldn't help but admire what it took to make the trek.

Without saying a word he grabbed a gunwale and helped yank the canoe free of the water. His scarred hands were the size of catcher's mitts, with knuckles as big as pine knots. Evidently the old man was no stranger to hard, physical work, and I wondered if he might be a retired farmer from Sanborn. But he wore the kind of knee-high leather boots that turn-of-the-century outdoorsmen used to wear, and an ancient, weather-worn, floppy campaign hat.

He nodded at the water in my canoe. "Saw you take that drop back there," he said. "Pretty fancy."

"Pretty lucky," I replied. I put my fishing gear on the ledge and flipped over the canoe for it to drain.

He pointed at my gear. "Come to fish this ledge, eh?"

I shrugged, hesitant to give anything away. "They say there's some nice browns in here—if you hit it right."

"Do they?" He was grinning.

I nearly laughed at the old-timer's quizzical smile. We both knew we were fencing, prying to discover how much the other knew about The Rock. My disappointment at finding the man ebbed when I thought about that. If the secret places along my river had to be known by another, I was glad to see he was someone who guarded them as I did.

"Where did you put in?" he asked.

"Maple Ridge Bridge."

He nodded and smiled again, his stubble of white whiskers glistening in the light. "Nice run, eh? Used to make it myself, back before they put the dam in near Sanborn. The White was really something then—all quickwater."

"She's still a nice stretch of water, though," I said.

"What's that, son? Oh, yes. Yes, she's a looker, all right." He scratched his cheek and turned upstream, staring at the rapids I had just come through. "I used to camp on this ledge when I was a youngster. Used to come here and watch the trout jump through that chute. They were all brook trout in those days, all two-pounders and better. There were Indians, too. They'd come in spring to spear suckers and pike—big pike."

I secured the canoe's painter and followed the man to where his gear lay on the ledge. He had a brittle cane rod with a primitive reel wound with a frayed, fabric line. At the end was a galvanized hook.

"Having any luck?" I asked.

"Not yet. Too early. You got to wait til the sun starts dropping and the brush wolves howl. When those little wolves start calling, you know the browns will bite." He looked up at the sky where the sun was falling away to the southwest. "Two, three hours, then the serious fishing starts. Hand me that gunnysack, eh?"

I picked up a wet burlap bag lying near my feet. There was a little weight to it, and it smelled of fish. The old man reached inside and pulled out a dead chub. He cut the small fish in half, tossed away the head, and impaled the tail end on his hook.

"My bait bucket," he said, nodding at the sack. "My creel, too. I'll be eighty-four come Armistice Day. At my age you don't go traipsing through the woods carrying a lot of paraphernalia."

I thought about the chance he had taken, coming alone through the woods at his age and in his shape. I imagined how he must have groped for his way along the shadow of an old logging trail, bucking hazelbrush and thorn thickets, crawling under windfalls and over rocks, enduring gnats, flies, and mosquitoes. The White must have meant a lot to him.

He cast to where the red, muddy water pillowed over a sub-merged boulder. A Muddler could always find a brown lurking behind that rock, and I wondered how really intimate the old man might be with my stream. A fish struck on the second cast, and the old-timer whooped like a boy. I then saw that he was shuffling dangerously near the lip of the ledge. He tottered there, like an old tree waiting to fall, his stiff, unsteady legs quivering like bowstrings. I was sure he was going to tumble in and I got behind him, ready to grab him.

But he survived the battle and reeled in a 14-inch brown, fat, bright, and shiny.

"Nice one," I said, admiring his catch.

"He's a runt," the old man said. He winked at me. "Let's put him back and see if we can't get his big brother."

I thought he was joking—even on the White, a 14-incher is something to brag about. But he released the fish, then put aside his rod and pulled a tin of tobacco from a pocket. "Smoke?" he asked.

We sat under a cedar and rolled our cigarettes. The old man took off his Smokey Bear hat and wiped his snowy head with a sleeve. He was trembling.

"I never get used to it," he said. "I've caught a million trout in my life, but each one is like the first." Then he leaned toward me and confided in a whisper, "They turn me into goddamn jelly."

He leaned back against the ragged bole of the cedar, looking out at the water. "Used to come here every spring for trout," he said. "Used to come by canoe, like you, til it got to be too much for me. Started walking in after that, but it was never the same. Today's the first time I've been back in here since—hell, I can't remember."

He fell silent and watched the stream. He was there, beside me, but when I saw the way he looked at the White I knew he was far away.

"Arnie—that's my boy—he's retired two years now and living in Arizona," the old man said. "Wants I should come live with him and his wife. Got an extra room for me and everything. Says I'm getting so I can't remember to put my pants on in the morning." The old-timer plucked a shred of tobacco from his lip and flicked it at the river. "Arizona! Now ain't that a helluva place for a woodtick like me to end up?"

I felt as if I should say something, but there was nothing to say. At the end of all the words nothing would have changed: the old man was going to Arizona.

"I wanted to see the White just one more time," he told me. "Wanted to come back in here and visit some memories. I was a skidder in the first camp that logged off her pine, almost seventy years ago. Handled a team of logging horses as big as dinosaurs. Should've seen the White then—she sparkled like champagne and her bluffs were solid white pine, trees as tall as church steeples and big around as poker tables."

He stopped, abruptly, looking out past the stream, and I knew he was in that faraway place again. He was someplace where the White still flowed like champagne, where the brook trout went two pounds and Indians speared pike and he was a young lumberjack handling a team of dinosaurs.

"First time I ran the White was in 1915," he said suddenly. "A timber cruiser got tangled up with a she-bear, and had to get himself to the sawbones up in Ashland. It was spring, and we couldn't get a wagon through the woods—the clay roads were like quicksand. Borrowed a birch bark canoe from an Indian camp, and I floated him down to the flag stop near Deer Creek.

From there we hitched a ride into town on a logging train. He came out all right—lived to marry three wives—but he never went near a canoe again." The old man laughed.

"That chute nearly killed us both," he said. The old man nodded upstream, at the drop where I had almost swamped. "After all this time, I can still feel what it was like to race with the White."

"There's nothing else like it," I said.

He nodded. "No, nothing else ever came close."

I looked upstream then, trying to see the river as the old man was seeing it. Maybe it was the way the fading light struck the stream, but suddenly the muddy water turned bright and clear, while the red-clay cliffs rose to a forest of towering pines. I could see the brook trout leaping upstream through the chute, and Indians poised with their spears, waiting for the run of northern pike. I heard the White rumbling from a mile away through the woods, while a young man in knee-high leather boots and a crisp campaign hat raced a thaw-swollen river in a birch bark canoe. It was as if I were looking at a river I didn't know, a stream as unfamiliar to me as a distant world. It was still the White River but now it was not mine; for at least a while longer it belonged to the old man at my side.

"Did you say something?" he suddenly asked. The old-timer had nodded off and now he was coming around. "Listen!"

I could hear the sad, lonesome call of a distant brush wolf. The coyote's wistful wail was like an echo from out of the past.

The old man squeezed my arm. "Hear that? Hear that?" The old eyes flashed with life and excitement. In them I caught something of the young man who had raced the White in another spring.

"She'll be dark in an hour," he said. "Get your outfit. There's plenty of room for two of us to fish from this ledge."

I looked at him, trying to decide if he really wanted me to stay. "Guess I started out too late," I told him. "I wanted to make the dam before dark."

He looked at me closely, like someone wiping away the dust before peering into an old mirror. Maybe he was trying to decide something, too. "Ever fish below the last rapids before the dam?" he asked.

I said I hadn't.

He winked at me. "Try it tonight."

I gathered my gear and pushed off in the canoe, waving to him as I passed.

I looked back and saw him casting. Then, just before the bend and swift water, I looked back once more and saw the rod was gone and that he was simply standing on The Rock, looking out at his river. Then the current caught the canoe, and all my thoughts turned to running the White. Ahead lay that part of the stream only a fool would dare run in the dark. But the brush wolves were calling, and a full moon was rising. It was going to be a fine night for racing with the White.

FIVE

The Rune of Loons

In the lake country where my cabin sits, the surest sign of spring's return is the wild, mad calling of loons. When the snow is all but gone and the first leads of open water appear, loons suddenly arrive and fill the woods with their yodeling. Inexplicably, these black-and-white checkerboard birds return each year on the very day the ice goes out. How the loons forecast that date is a mystery.

Mystery and runes have long been associated with loons. To the old Norsemen, runes were secret, mystical songs that, if deciphered, would answer every riddle. More than one Viking sought life's answers in the eerie cry of loons—a trembling and ghostly wail that sounds like *Who are you?*

That sound is as much a part of the North as are the trees and rocks. The twilight tolling of loons reminds me of all the places I've known throughout the North—of haunted and mysterious lands swaddled in moonlight, of ebony lakes and shimmering black rivers, and of lonesome campsites deep in the wilderness teeming with magic as loons began to call. It also conjures images of a time when we were more like beasts than men.

The oldest and most primitive of all northern water birds, loons do not belong to the same family as ducks and geese. Instead, they most closely resemble fossils. Vikings believed loon calls were the wails of lost souls. The Cree and Chippewa thought of loons as supernatural messengers. And in the days before radio and radar, mariners on the Great Lakes listened for loon calls when approaching fogbound shores to keep from running aground. In one way or another, people have long looked to loons for direction.

I'm skeptical of remote lakes where loons are absent, especially if I'm fishing and not getting strikes. There are tens of thousands of lakes all across the Canadian Shield that, for one reason or another, hold no fish. Loons—which feed on fish— avoid these lakes. Whenever I'm on unfamiliar water without a guide or fish locator, I listen for loon calls before investing too much time in fishing these places.

Loons can also reveal the presence of large predator fish. In early spring, pike and loons feed on the same schools of baitfish. I've often followed loons to locate feeding pike. And in summer, the biggest muskies lurk near nests that hold loon chicks.

I was a boy when I first learned about loons from Hjalmer Maki. Hjalmer was one of those old-time, backwoods, Scandinavian hermits whose tar-paper shacks used to dot the roadless woods of northern Wisconsin. Hjalmer's shack stood on what was then a seldom-visited lake. Just before sunrise, when the wind was still and white mists galloped out of the bays, loons would gather off the point in front of Hjalmer's shack to fill the dawn with their calling. Their quivering cries were so plangent and shrill that the land itself seemed to quake. Eventually the loons would swim away in pairs, until only one old bird remained. The call of this bird was a low, long wail. This solitary bird was Hjalmer's favorite.

"I think it's because I understand what the bird is sayin'," Hjalmer once told me. "He's old and lonely, he's got nobody and nothing, and he knows time is gettin' short but he still ain't figured things out."

"What kind of things?" I asked.

Hjalmer shrugged and looked away. "Seems like somebody set us down here for some reason, but I never met nobody who could tell me why."

Like the northern lights or a hunter's moon, I took loons for granted until they began disappearing from places that were once full of their calling. One of these places is Green Bass Lake. When I knew it, Green Bass was a crystalline jewel of wilderness water whose solitude was still undisturbed. As a boy, it was where I went when I wanted to be alone.

One year I came to Green Bass just as the ice was going out, while the country was still cold and colorless, and the trees sere and stark. At dusk the lakeshore's flooded grasses were filled with the din of spring peepers. Out on the lake beaver tails slapped the water and far to the north brush wolves howled. But all my attention was fixed on the lake's loons.

I stood on a hill at sunset, watching as a pair of loons moved across the lake. They were an image of grace, gliding soundlessly across an amber lake full of reflections. Then darkness fell as though it were dropped from the sky, the moon climbed above the timber, and the lake swelled with the loons' call, *Who are you?*

It was a wild, eerie yodeling and I shuddered at the sound. Soon, loons on the nearby lakes answered. In an instant the spare, spring landscape echoed with loon calls. Then the yodeling reached a high, screaming pitch, a mad mix of yowls and maniacal laughter that turned my spit cold. And yet I felt a sense of peace and well-being that I had never known before. That night, standing beside Green Bass Lake and listening to the wild calling clearly, I knew that this was the place where I longed to belong.

Nowadays, a lifetime later, I walk away from the day's cares come sunset, and I visit the lake below my cabin. This is the quiet part of the day when the world is hushed and the slow approach of night exerts its calm. The loons on the lake seem to know it and become more purposeful in their calling, while I grow more aware of being there, aloof and alone.

This is the time when thoughts are free to meander; yet I try not to think at all. If anything, I may pause to inspect a pebble lying on the beach where glaciers dropped it ten thousand years ago, and marvel that the stone has lain there all this time, waiting to be discovered by me. Or I may consider the ancient light of the constellations, fascinated by the thought that they shine as brightly for me as they did for the first man. Meanwhile, the loons continue calling as their kind always has, *Who are you?* I peer into the water and am startled by the image of a stranger.

In the purpling dusk the shadows grow longer. The lake reflects the dimming light, and in the gathering dark the loon calls wane. Reluctant to leave, I stand and listen, waiting for a last hint of loon music—a rune I understand but cannot explain.

SIX

Reefer Creek

It begins as a tea-colored trickle in a spruce bog near Lake Superior, and for most of its length it is much too small to take a fly. It has no rapids, no waterfalls, no stands of stunning timber, and its narrow places are a snarl of beaver slash and windfalls. A few native brook trout haunt its alder-choked pools, but no serious angler ever wets a line there; for in a land laced with gemstone rivers like the White, the Namekagon, and Bois Brule, Reefer Creek is an ordinary stream that other fishermen ignore.

Still, the Reefer is a special place for me. I know its moods, its changes, its fluctuations, as well as every riffle and rock. And sometimes, when I've been away from it too long, I catch myself daydreaming—imagining myself working my way through every pool. For whether I visit it in waders or by wizardry, the Reefer is my secret place and it is with me always, its images tucked safely away in memory, like thumbworn photos in a wallet.

The Reefer's hold on me began soon after I moved to the Lake Superior country, when I was barely out of my teens. Old John, our local backwoods recluse, took it upon himself to reveal to me the magic of wild trout. In those days my fishing outfit consisted of a fiberglass rod and a Heddon spinning reel, and a modest collection of spinners and spoons. John took one look at my gear and shook his head.

"I take it you're not a trout fishermen," he said. "We're going to have to do something about that."

One day he came to call with his fly-fishing outfit: a primitive cane rod, a reel of unknown vintage, and a Prince Albert Tobacco pocket tin filled with a few flies and a tattered spare leader. His old outfit was as poor as my own, but I saw from the start what it meant to him. John's legs had been crippled in a logging accident, and it had been years since he'd waded a stream; but as he taught me how to cast a fly, the cane rod worked like a magic wand, and John was once again the man he used to be.

One evening we fished Reefer Creek at the place he called High Banks. John's twisted legs kept him from climbing down the steep clay banks to the water, but he was satisfied to sit beneath the balsams at the top of the bank. From there he coached and cheered me on, laughing each time I gave a shout when a smallish trout took the fly and burst from the pool.

After a while I scrambled up the bank and showed John his creel: three fish were lying on a bed of sphagnum, the tiny brookies barely bigger than fingerlings, but each a thing of joy and beauty.

"They all took the Black Gnat," I told him, "just like you said they would."

John looked at the trout and nodded. "Hmm, nice ones."

I held his cane rod in the air, like the staff of a banner. "Boy, I'd give anything to own a rod like this."

"Then it's yours," John said. "The reel and bugs, too. I can't use them anymore, and I'll be dammed if they go to hell with the rest of me."

I looked at him, too young to fully appreciate the depth of his gesture, yet aware that something important was happening. The world had robbed John of his greatest passion, and the loss would have turned another man malevolent and mean. But that night, listening to him hoot and laugh as I battled the Reefer's tiny trout with his timeworn gear, I sensed for the first time why life's enduring joys have nothing to do with getting and taking.

Years later I often fished the Reefer with Finnish Bill. Bill was a quiet man, silent and shy, and the only place he ever fished along the Reefer was the spot known as the Singapore Pool.

The Singapore is a wide bulge in the stream, bordered by rock ledges and twin colonnades of old cedars that lean over the water to form a roof above the creek. It's a dark place of shadows where sunlight seldom enters, and even in the hottest weather the black water has the feel of ice.

Sometimes, after I left him to work my way far downstream, I'd return hours later to the Singapore and find Bill standing in the same place where I had last seen him. Bill seldom knew I was near at such times, and I would watch as he remained rooted in the current, casting time and again to where he had seen a rise, never changing patterns, and sure that sooner or later a fish would strike. Almost always, Bill left the Reefer with an empty creel.

One day I walked to the Singapore and saw Bill standing at the head of the pool, making cast after cast to a good rise below him. He was oblivious of my presence, and I watched as he dropped the fly into the window, and then I heard the splash as a broadtail broke water. Bill cast again, unnerved. This time the fly vanished in a swirl.

From the way the rod buckled I could tell Bill had tied into one of the Reefer's real trout. The fish tried to gain the muddy bank below the ledges, where the cedars stopped and alders began, but Bill turned the fish away from the tangles, and soon the trout was slicing small circles in the current. Bill dipped his net, and when he brought it up he was holding the largest trout I had ever seen on Reefer Creek.

The brookie glistened in the single shaft of sunlight that pierced the cedars' crown. It was better than sixteen inches, mossy-green on top, speckled with red and blue along the sides, with a belly as bright as a hot copper penny. I would have given a whole season of trout fishing to catch a prize like that. I thought I was hallucinating when Bill released the fish.

"Are you crazy?" I called, stepping out of the trees, into the open where Bill could see me.

He looked at me and grinned, like a kid caught taking a bite from an apple before tossing it back into the bin.

"Why did you let him go?" I asked.

Bill waded over to me and winked. "He was too big for my creel," Bill said. "Besides, this place just wouldn't be the same without him."

It undoubtedly was a beautiful trout, but I saw now that the fishing was only an excuse for Bill to visit Reefer Creek. The real catch was the hours Bill could spend alone at Singapore Pool, with its dark, brooding water, its rocky ledges and ageless cedars, and its sense of isolation, solitude, and peace. The trout was part of these things but it wasn't *everything*, and when I looked at the Singapore now it was as though I had never really seen Reefer Creek.

One year, at the very end of the season, I fished the Reefer with Rick, my closest friend. The water was low and fishing had been poor even on good streams like the Siskiwit and Sioux, but it was the last chance we would have to spend time together in the outdoors. The company Rick worked for was promoting him, and in a few days he was being transferred to the East Coast.

We talked about keeping in touch, and maybe getting together once he was settled in Philadelphia, but we both knew it was all a lie. Our years of sharing trout streams, duck blinds, and deer camps were over: all that remained was this last day at Reefer Creek.

We worked the Reefer slowly. In the good places I fell behind to let him make the first cast, and in the better places Rick always found some excuse why I should have the first crack at a pool. I had Rick's going-away gift wrapped in tissue and stashed on a closet shelf, and later there would be the farewell party with others in a crowded room. But we both knew Reefer Creek would be where our real good-byes were said, and neither of us was in any hurry to reach the end of the stream.

When we came out to where the creek empties into Lake Superior, I peeled away my hip boots and sat down on a log at the beach, watching as Rick kept casting to a rise that was never there. He worked slowly and purposefully, knowing that each cast might be the last. Then the sun began to set and with it the lake mists turned the Reefer into a ribbon of smoking glass. The only welt on the water was the coil of Rick's line.

"Well, I guess that's it," he said.

We put the fishing gear aside and watched the sunset, listening to the final trilling of white-throats and warblers. Then it was time to leave and we took a last look at things, like tourists who know they will not be coming back next year, or the year after that, or ever again.

As trout streams go, the Reefer is at the bottom of most anglers' lists, but for me every pool is a memory of someone I used to know. Time has scattered my old friends like dry leaves, but when I wade Reefer Creek I am never alone.

SEVEN

Stormbound

One of the hazards of fishing the North Country is getting caught out in the open when bad weather strikes. At times I'm able to wait out such storms in a tent or cabin, but far more often I've had to make do with what was at hand.

As a result, I have waited out storms under rock ledges, inside caves, beneath windfalls, and in the dry spots under trees. Some people consider being stormbound in such places an ordeal, but for me, every one of these shelters has felt as familiar as a room I once lived in long ago.

One time, while fishing alone on an isolated stretch of the North Branch of the Oconto River, I was surprised by a sudden squall. I had paddled my canoe far upstream against the current, too intent on fishing to heed the gathering signs in the sky. At noon the wind changed direction, and daylight disappeared as low, black clouds moved swiftly out of the southwest. I turned the canoe and began paddling back toward camp, trying to make the tent before the storm broke.

It was hopeless. Behind me lightning was leaping from cloud to cloud, and thunder grew in intensity and violence. Heavy raindrops pelted the river like birdshot, while birches along the banks cracked like whips in the wind.

I turned toward the bank and a stand of hemlocks. Dragging the canoe up into the trees, I flipped it over and propped up one of the gunwales on a pair of forked sticks. Then, using my jacket for a pillow, I crawled under the makeshift lean-to, lay down on a blanket of wintergreen, and remained on my side while the storm passed overhead.

Although a tent or cabin would have been welcomed, their walls would have shut out more than weather and wind. Under the canoe I was close to the elements and as much a part of the landscape as I have ever been.

It's this sense of belonging that primitive storm shelters stir. When you're trapped by the weather beneath a windfall or rock shelf, such places seem to rekindle an old warmth and ancient intimacy. Perhaps they touch something lost by modern man—the time when caverns and caves were the only shelter available. Primitive men spent much time in such places, and these sites have left an indelible mark upon us. You see it in children when they build crude, cardboard houses, and when they are drawn to the constant twilight of culverts and hollow logs. These places are filled with mysteries and adventures, and though we grow older, the lure of their magic never fades.

Some years ago I recaptured that magic on an isolated island in Lake Superior. Once it had been a bustling base camp for French explorers and fur traders, but by the time I discovered it, the island had the weathered look of a land both forgotten and forlorn.

One afternoon, while fishing for giant pike near the mouth of a stream, a lake storm rushed over the island with the sudden fury of a cataract. The wind hurled aspens through space as if they were jackstraws, and the earth rocked and heaved as things crashed to the ground.

I hid under a sandstone ledge concealed by mature cedars. It jutted out from the high bank of the stream, the entrance obscured by the tentacle roots of old trees. From there, I watched as birches across the river flickered in the lightning. Then I noticed the mound of old ashes and charcoal just inside the entrance. Apparently, I was not the first traveler to take shelter under the ledge.

Without thinking about it, I picked up a stick and began scratching through the ashes. Obviously, no one had built a fire at that spot in ages, but at one time the ledge had been a favorite resting place. Perhaps it had been a campsite of early woodsmen and trappers who traveled light and depended upon natural shelters at the end of the day. But I was surprised to see layers of charcoal extending deeper than a dozen inches—it would have taken countless years for ashes to accumulate to that depth.

I began wondering if the ledge had sheltered stormbound fur traders when lake gales and high winds had pinned their fragile craft to shore. I wondered, too, if the Chippewa and Ottawa had gathered there in a time before the first French explorers, fleeing winds and rains, and listening to the Hurons' tales of great, white giants in the east. A minute later I had my answer: deep in the ashes I unearthed an arrowhead.

Suddenly I felt close to the wild in a way I had not felt before. Here, in the cleft of the rocks, I had found a place outside of time. For unknown centuries the ledge had sheltered Indians and explorers, voyageurs and woodsmen; and now it sheltered a modern-day sojourner. Although there was an immense gulf between those early travelers and myself, our needs and instincts were not affected by the years. A simple rock shelter was as important to me as it had been for them. Here was a sense of intimacy and familiarity—it was like going back to some point in time and finding out nothing had changed.

Another time, along another river, I was pinned in by the weather for several days. I had come to the secluded stream with the idea of catching wilderness brookies—all twelve inches and better. A friend had promised me the use of a trapper's cabin, so I had traveled light and had not packed a tent. But the cabin turned out to be nothing more than a crude lean-to built of aspen logs, spruce boughs, and bark.

It rained for three days—a cold, constant, steady, gray drizzle that stripped the leaves from the trees and made lighting a match a nearly impossible task. The river flooded, its islands vanished, and streamside trails turned to ooze. The only brookies I caught were diminutive trout barely longer than a finger. I could never have imagined a more miserable and dreary place; yet, by crawling inside the lean-to, I escaped to a different land.

Under the low-slung roof of birch bark and spruce boughs, the anxiety I felt about being stormbound was made to seem unimportant and less real. Inside those squat, rugged log walls, it seemed enough to just be there, alone in a wild place, far from the day-to-day problems of a confusing world. Life at the lean-to was elemental; my most pressing concerns were catching fish for supper and keeping the matches out of the rain. At night, when the coyotes yodeled from the misty ridges, it seemed that a campfire and a dry spot were all the comforts I would ever need.

The wild is always calling in such places. Like camping beside an open fire deep in the wilderness, they satisfy an old hunger for a primitive world. To some, being stormbound in a crude and natural shelter may be a cheerless trial; but for me, such places always have the familiar look of old friends I used to know.

EIGHT

Spring Cleaning

My friend Roger would be the perfect outdoor companion except for one irritating habit—he's *neat*. He's the kind of fussy,
finicky, fastidious sort of person who does annoying things like
putting back stuff where it belongs.

After cleaning a fish, he puts his fillet knife back in the tackle
box, instead of leaving it behind on a log. At home he keeps his
fishing rods stored in cases, instead of dumping them into a corner with a lot of other junk.

If Roger and I are steelhead fishing the Brule River, Roger
will have all steelhead hooks in his pockets, instead of the pot-
pourri of fish hooks I usually find in mine. He's the sort of
person who buys fishing tackle at a sport show in January, and
actually remembers what he did with it when May arrives.

I'm especially annoyed with Roger because I'm in the midst
of spring cleaning and realize that my fishing gear is in utter dis-
array. The next time I go fishing and need a stringer, it'll be much
easier to just go out and buy one instead of trying to find any of
the dozen I already own.

At home, the spare bedroom that serves as my den is packed,
the closets are full, and the garage is jammed to the rafters. My

basement is a maze of unmarked trails through boxes, bags, and piles of outdoor gear. In a way, I feel sorry for people like Roger—there's no sense of adventure in their orderly lives. Each time I enter my basement it's like setting out in search of the undiscovered; if you visit Roger's cellar you'll only find a furnace.

Last winter Roger invited me into his basement to look at some flies he had tied, but except for his tidy fly-tying workbench, there was no hint that an angler lived in that house. There was no sign of worn-out waders, rusty bait buckets, splintered canoe paddles, or broken fishing rods. I guess neat people don't like to clutter up their lives with a lot of memories.

Among my most cherished possessions is a collection of hip boots. I own one pair of feet and five hip boots. Two leak, two are too small, and one was set too close to a campfire. But I'm not the sort of a man who discards old friends. Besides, you never know when the missing boot might turn up. If it does, its story will rival that of the phoenix.

Roger throws away broken fishing reels and those near-empty jars that hold one, last, single salmon egg. Not me. I'm holding on to the reels in case the missing pieces turn up, or if the companies that made them go back into business and resume the manufacturing of odd-sized screws no one else ever thought to machine. And one of these days I'm going to empty all my lonely salmon eggs into one jar just in time for steelhead season. I'll save a fortune in bait—or at least a $1.98.

If I ever begin to tidy up my life, tossing out my old books would be a good place to start. Like most fishermen, I'm always eager to add to my store of outdoor knowledge, and so I regularly buy books guaranteed to help me master some facet of the sporting life.

They never do.

Understanding Wild Trout was just as hard to understand as trout were in the first place.

A Beginner's Guide to Canoeing wasn't much help either. The author's canoe may be "responsive," but the ones I've known are just plain tippy.

But nothing is more difficult than parting with a book, even if it's a bad one. In fact, I can barely bring myself to toss out my fishing magazines. So I don't.

It's not that I'm hesitant to throw things out—it's simply that what other people see as junk is usually a priceless memento to me. My old, red shirt is an example. I was wearing that shirt when I caught my first legal muskie thirty years ago, and I continue to wear it whenever I fish for muskies. The elbows are gone, the sleeves are too short, and for the last ten years the buttons only fasten at a single juncture across my chest. Recently, I've been getting a lot of new fishing shirts as gifts, but you don't part with something as lucky as my old, red rag. I've worn that shirt for thirty seasons now, and in that time I've caught three legal muskies. Shirts don't get any luckier than that.

Maybe I'm just better at saving junk than I am at money, but that isn't all bad. Someday, after Roger and I are gone, his kids may argue over the cash in his perfectly balanced checkbook. I doubt if anyone will squabble over my estate. Of course, it's always possible the family may have a falling out over who gets to keep my lucky red shirt. Maybe I'll make a will and leave it to my wife. She's always looked good in red.

PART TWO

SUMMER

NINE

Abbey Lake

I first visited Abbey Lake thirty years ago, just after I made the Lake Superior country my home. The Abbey Lake area was still wilderness then, as was much of northern Wisconsin—a place where people and "No Trespassing" signs were as rare as two-headed trout. I made the short hike in from Lake Number One, coming down through the scrub oak and jack-pine along an old logging trail on the south side of Abbey. It was early June and largemouth bass were only beginning to stake out their spawning beds.

The land dropped sharply as I neared Abbey Lake. The sandy earth was covered in a slick mat of last year's dried oak leaves, and I had to hold onto saplings to keep from sliding down the hill. I took the last twenty feet in a headlong rush after tripping over a log. Only the thick stand of bulrushes at the bottom of the hill stopped me from landing in the lake.

I was startled by the clarity of Abbey Lake. Its water was as transparent as a windowpane, its sand bottom white as sugar. Nothing but ripple marks marred the flawless sand—not a stone, or a shell, or a twig. The hardstem bulrushes were the only vegetation I could see. Like most of the lakes that lie between the

St. Croix and Eau Claire Rivers, the infertile, sandy soil of the surrounding jack-pine barrens produces gin-clear lakes that are empty of nutrients. The result is a weedless, almost oligotrophic lake populated by bluegills and a few big bass.

It was during that first visit to Abbey that I saw what I still call "The King Bass," though it was probably a pre-spawn female swollen with eggs. I stood there at the edge of the bulrushes, checking my gear to make sure I hadn't snapped off my rod tip, and that my trout knife was still tucked in my back pocket in case a fish—or a bear—happened along.

A bald eagle was aloft above the lake. In the lake's southeast bay, a mallard hen sat motionless on a nest built upon an island of mud and beaver slash. Somewhere a loon was yodeling, and I was trying to locate the bird when I saw (or sensed) motion near my feet. I looked down.

In the bulrushes, three feet out from shore and in barely a foot of water, swam a largemouth bass the size of my dog. The largest bass I've *ever* caught in Wisconsin was twenty-two inches long, and this fish was larger than that.

It was high noon, but the sky was obscured by dark clouds: I think that's why the bass didn't dart away—it simply didn't see me. I was trembling like a tuning fork, shaking so badly that I twice dropped the Weedless Minnow I was trying to tie to my line. All the while the bass lay there, finning, gills flapping, moving a foot off to my right and then stopping, before beginning the entire process again. A shaft of sunlight broke through the clouds when I finally raised my arm to cast; as I did, the rod's shadow struck the fish. The bass bolted like lightning, speeding away into deep water. I never saw it again.

For years afterward I'd daydream about going back to Abbey Lake and catching that fish. Every time I was in the area I'd make a little side trip to Abbey, even in winter, and think about the bass under the ice, growing bigger. Female largemouths rarely live ten years in the North and the fish I saw must have been older than that. Yet even after enough time had passed that I knew it was gone, I still thought about the King Bass, and secretly hoped to return to Abbey Lake and by some miracle find the fish waiting for me in the bulrushes. "Hope is the last thing that dies in a man," wrote La Rochefoucauld, "and though it be exceedingly deceitful, yet it is of this good use to us, that while traveling through life it conducts us in an easier and more pleasant way to our journey's end."

*   *   *

The jack-pine forests of northwestern Wisconsin teem with solitude and largemouth bass. Covering a quarter-million acres and speckled with thousands of lakes, much of this wilderness goes unvisited—in fact, most of its lakes have never been named.

Secret Lake is typical of this area's small bass lakes. "Secret" is only what I call it—on maps, it appears as an anonymous spot of blue. It lies on public land near the Eau Claire River. Barely twenty acres in size and fifteen feet deep, its undeveloped shoreline is solidly timbered in pine. Access is by way of an old logging trail. Like most jack-pine lakes, there is no boat landing; a canoe or waders are essential.

Like Abbey Lake, Secret Lake is also typical in that it has a sandy bottom, no algae, few weeds, little structure, and water as transparent—and as chemically pure—as rain. This is why casual anglers never return to the jack-pines: the flawless water clarity makes for skittish fish that can be difficult to catch.

The day I visited Secret Lake, I peered down through eight feet of crystal clear water at hefty largemouths finning against the lake's sugar-sand bottom—but at the sight of my canoe, the fish scattered. Bass in these clear lakes feel unprotected in direct sun-light, and on sunny days they head for the deepest water avail-able. Yet with the approach of sunset, you can catch dozens of largemouths on a popper right from shore.

Diminishing light is the key to enticing bass in the jack-pines. Whether it be actual dusk or the "false twilight" created by cloud cover, the lower light levels bass associate with feeding draw them out of deep water and into the shallows, where they are eas-ier to find and catch.

Just a few days ago a friend and I fished one of the countless unnamed lakes near the crossroads known as Wascott. The little pool of icy clear water was said to be brimming with three-pound largemouths. But though we fished from sunrise to noon, all we took were undersized fish. Then, just after lunch, the sky turned gunmetal gray as clouds moved in ahead of a storm. Without warning, big bass began striking our Rapalas.

Raindrops pelted us like hailstones. Wind bent trees as if they were twigs. Finally, when distant thunder rumbled, we pointed our canoe toward shore. But during those first few min-utes of the storm, we caught and released more than a dozen de-cent bass.

Bass in these lakes—like most fish in the North—are gluttons when it rains. Worms gets washed into the water, insects float along the shore, and baitfish start moving. With all this food sud-denly there for the taking, bass become opportunists—they strike at the largest meal they can swallow. After rain, fish against the shore with the wind in your face. Jig-and-leech rigs and minnow imitations, like Rapalas or Mepps Comets, work best.

Bass fishing can be cyclic in the jack-pines. Fish populations crashed after several harsh winters in the 1990s, but thanks to unseasonably mild winters since then, bass numbers are exploding; in fact, largemouths now are found in lakes where they were historically absent. Two-pound bass are common; seven pounders can turn up in the biggest lakes. Until a winter of excessively deep snows and subzero temperatures strikes, the best fishing is yet to come.

Resource biologists describe lakes like Abbey and Secret as being "mildly mesotrophic," meaning they are not as sterile as the purely oligotrophic lakes commonly found farther north. Consequently, bass grow bigger and faster here than they do in less fertile water.

Wisconsin's jack-pine barrens are a transitional zone, a sort of vestibule to the real North. Immediately south of the jack-pines is a land of swales, marsh, oak groves, and prairies. North of the St. Croix's headwaters, the jack-pines give way to spruce, lakes are replaced by streams, and the bass yield their place at the top of the aquatic food chain to pike and trout. Wisconsin's jack-pines barrens are at the northern limit of the largemouth's native range.

Most of the lakes lie on public or commercial forest lands. All are open to the public. But not all lakes hold bass—some are just too shallow. Many good lakes lie near Barnes and the Eau Claire River; lakes between the St. Croix and Totagatic Rivers are also sure bets. Even as far south as the headwaters of the Clam River you can find extraordinary bass lakes. Topographical maps are necessary to find the most remote water.

Be aware you're on your own here—some lakes go unvisited for years. Access trails are poor, and after a rain they can be washed out or blocked by falling timber. Occasionally, fishermen enter these woods and are never heard from again. Whether you find that frightening or fascinating will determine the size of the bass you catch here.

*   *   *

I found Abbey Lake exactly as I had left it. The miles of wilderness that once insulated it were no longer quite as vast, but the hike in to Abbey was still a lonely, physical effort. I came to it at dusk last night, the air filled with the whining of insects and the croaking of frogs. It was warm enough to wade the shallows in old running shoes and shorts; beyond the bulrushes, bass as big as logs occasionally broke the surface, chasing damsel-flies and frogs.

I made a few casts with a Hula Popper, but found I had no patience to fish it properly, which is letting the lure lay motionless on the surface for a minute or two before beginning a slow and agonizing start-and-stop retrieve. Hula Poppers are perfect lures for lazy summer evenings, but I was feeling too anxious to be composed.

I switched to a Jitterbug. On ten casts I caught three bass, little fish of a pound or so. All went back. If you visit the jack-pine lakes during the day, the sun-shy fish can make you believe that bass don't exist. But after dark it's difficult not to catch fish on the topwater. The traditional red-and-white pattern of old-time lures seem to work best. I like that as much as I do anything about the jack-pines' bass. It's nice to know that some things are timeless.

La Rochefoucauld aside, I had no illusions—the King Bass was gone, but maybe it had left behind an heir. I made a few dozen casts with the Jitterbug.

Nothing.

An hour later a bat swooped past my face, nearly knocking me over. Bass were jumping in front of the bulrushes, a few of them good sized. But I was hunting Leviathan.

Another forty casts. Still nothing.

It's not that I need to catch big bass to enjoy bass fishing. But it is comforting to know that the monsters are there—not the monsters that haunt your restless, sleepless nights at 3:00 A.M., but the kind that festoon the walls of the old North's bait shops and saloons.

A dozen more casts. Nothing.

The sunset's afterglow was gone and Venus was blazing. Sane people were at home asleep in their beds. And all I had was a little pocket flashlight to find my way back through the darkening woods. The thought of what might be lurking in those woods started me thinking about other kinds of monsters—the sort of malignities that stalk the darksome forests of disappointment: the best friend whose treachery had taught me to hate; the litigious acquaintance whose lawsuit kept me awake at night; the neighbor who claimed the ferrules on my favorite rod were already crushed when I loaned it to him; and the fear that innocence and goodness were as much an anachronism as my red-and-white Jitterbug.

I reeled in the plug, cut the line with my teeth, and turned toward shore—just as a bass jumped beside me.

The fish jumped again, too long to completely clear the water. A five pounder, I thought. Maybe six.

It was too dark to see the end of my monofilament, and so I held the flashlight between my teeth as I rushed to tie the Jitterbug to my line. The plug hit the water with a splash, and perfidy vanished in a ring of ripples.

Slurp! Another bass broke the surface, inhaling a frog as big as a plum.

One fishes not to catch fish, but to be caught—caught up in the innocence and unsullied artlessness that is fishing. Here— where faith, hope, and expectation meet—I see a bass jump and know there is one thing on this earth that will never wound my affection. A few lines from Wordsworth seemed to sum up what I was feeling as I cast again to the jumping bass:

> And so I dare to hope,
> Though changed, no doubt, from what I was when first
> I came among these hills; when like a roe
> I bounded o'er the mountains, by the sides
> Of the deep rivers, and the lonely streams,
> Wherever nature led: more like a man
> Flying from something that he dreads, than one
> Who sought the thing he loved.

TEN

The Gloaming

An old Scotsman with whom I once fished called it "the gloam-ing," those few, fleeting moments between dusk and dark, when winds disappear, woods turn still as stone, loons begin to call, and lakes pool like quicksilver. It's the hour of mystery and magic, when anything can happen, and often does; it is the mo-ment when the looking-glass surface of a wilderness lake reflects more than shorelines and clouds.

At such times the world becomes a different place. Action gives way to abeyance, and all things slow to the pace of a dream. Whenever the gloaming strikes, I long to be on the flatwater, glid-ing through the gathering dusk in a silent canoe. For although the less adventuresome will begin huddling around the light of campfires, the gloaming seldom fails those who go fishing.

Once, on a big lake along the Minnesota-Ontario border, a west wind and whitecaps kept our canoe pinned to a rocky point for most of the day. But at sunset the wind vanished, and the treacherous combers turned to a tarn of level slate.

My partner and I rigged our rods and shoved off, gliding across the water with scarcely a ripple. We paddled over the im-age of a clouded copper sky, past shorelines where the tall spruce stood like steeples. A bass jumped in a nearby weedy bay, shattering the fragile quiet, and without either one of us having to say a word, my friend and I paddled toward the cove.

The bay was concealed by a wall of reeds and rushes, and as we neared we saw a large shadow rise from the shallows. We froze, thinking we had caught a black bear unaware, and let the momentum of our last stroke carry the canoe toward the darkening shore. At that moment, the setting sun broke through the clouds, its final, level rays gilding the shore with copper light; and there, in the shallows among the reeds, stood the largest moose either of us had ever seen.

The animal lifted its head. The sun struck its massive antlers, and the rack gleamed like foxfire in the dark. Then the sun found our canoe, illuminating the gunwales like twin rails of light, and for a moment we, too, were part of the mirage. The animal saw us and turned in the water, crashing through the shallows for shore. But soon the silence returned and the turbulence ebbed, and the lake once again lay calm.

My partner looked over his shoulder at me. "What did we just see?" he asked. He was stunned by the magic.

I knew what he meant, for I had felt the spell, too. It was the gloaming that had lured us to that bay, where we had seen more than just a sunset—or even a moose.

Since then I've experienced the gloaming many times and in many places, but it always shines brightest on the wilderness lakes of the North. Here, it can occur any time from ice-out to freeze-up; but it's at twilight during the long days of summer when the magic is most apparent. Whenever it strikes, the gloaming seldom lasts for more than a few minutes. Yet in those moments the impressions it leaves can often last a lifetime.

Early one summer I was fishing a bay on a large lake near Upper Michigan's primitive Sylvania area. The ice had gone out of the lakes only weeks before, and when the sun began to set the red sky had the look of winter. Suddenly the shallows began to slither and sputter, and when I looked I saw thousands of tiny, black, inch-long bullheads moving along the shoreline like a mile-long eel. From the spruce-clad shore a lone white-throat gave its pensive whistle, signaling the start of another gloaming as every gamefish in the bay went on the attack.

Bass jumped and splashed at the shore. I saw a swirl near a submerged pine stump and watched as a muskie leaped into the air. I tossed out a plug and took six bass on as many casts; minutes later I caught three walleyes. And then suddenly the light was gone, and with it went all the action that had made the bay come alive.

I turned the canoe and began paddling back to camp, cruising along avenues of mirrored moonbeams. The canoe slipped past pine-studded islands that loomed like battleships in the dark, while shorelines throbbed with the hunting calls of owls. I caught the swift whisper of wings overhead; it was a pair of loons, hurtling through the dark, and when they saw me the big birds cried out in alarm.

The shorelines echoed with the birds' lonely call, and instantly loons from other parts of the lake began to answer. In turn, birds from surrounding lakes answered those calls, and soon the night was filled with wild music. In the distance a pack of brush wolves began to howl, joining the haunting melody. Everywhere the endless echoes kept the calling alive, until it was impossible to distinguished the real from the copy.

I felt as though I had paddled through a gap in time, back to when men still used fire as a buckler against the night and the wild things calling in the darkness. I began to feel uncomfortably close to that distant past, but then the calling drifted off, and there was only the sound of my paddle in the water.

There's no way to know when the gloaming will strike, no way to prepare for its wizardry. But like a deer hunter patiently waiting on a stand beside a trail, I keep my ears and eyes open at dusk, knowing that—sooner or later—the magic will come.

One experience I had during the gloaming remains especially vivid. It was the end of August, and already the maples and sumac had turned bright as blood on the hillsides surrounding a tiny bog. The bog lay within earshot of Lake Superior, and as evening approached I could hear the sound of foghorns as ore boats moved through the lake's mists.

At dusk the pond turned into glimmer glass, mirroring the colors of its shore. Dry leaves that had been drifting like toy ships suddenly halted in the water; everything seemed to pause in the hush and calm.

A beaver splashed. An owl called. Wood ducks whistled overhead. And then the sky opened above Lake Superior to the north, and the brilliant streamers of the Northern Lights fell from the stars like a shimmering stage curtain.

It was the gloaming, certainly, but this was one of a kind. Everything I sought from the North Country seemed to be embodied in that singular moment: the wilderness lake, the stunning silence, the solitude and isolation, and the freedom of fishing from a canoe in a primitive and unspoiled land.

I felt bewitched as I cast a popper at the shore. A bass grabbed the lure in a pool of polar light, and when it jumped the spray sparkled like a shower of stardust. I released the fish and turned toward camp, paddling across the flatwater reflections. But it was as if I were no longer on the water at all, but in a canoe riding the rainbow rapids of the Aurora.

ELEVEN

Portage Trails

Every portage trail has a lure all its own, but the spell they weave is the same. They stir a sense of restlessness, an impatience with familiar routines, and a need to know what lies beyond where the eye can see. A barely discernible track, winding its way through wilderness toward some point that can only be guessed about, will tug at a man like a voice in a dream. For portages are more than just detours around rapids or links between lakes—each one is a bridge with yesterday.

Portage is a French word meaning "carrying place." It is the term early explorers gave to the overland routes that linked North America's lakes and rivers into a highway that spanned the length and breadth of the continent. Long before the first explorations of Cartier, Marquette, Joliet, and La Salle, Indians had used the trails for untold ages, but when Lake Superior became the hub of the fur trade in the late seventeenth century, the French quickly developed these portages into highly prized avenues of commerce.

From various outposts along the lake, the voyageurs set out to venture up whitewater rivers, trading European-made goods for furs harvested by Indians deep in the wilderness. For two hundred years these men paddled and portaged between Montreal and Lake Superior, and then north and westward as far as the Arctic and Pacific Oceans. Although their portage trails once existed throughout the continent, most have been erased by civilization. However, a few of the old trails still remain in wilderness areas of the North.

One of these is the Brule-St. Croix passage at the west end of Lake Superior. This two-mile-long trail connects the St. Croix and Bois Brule Rivers, providing the shortest natural route between Lake Superior and the Mississippi. It was discovered in 1680 by Daniel Greysolon, who had first believed he had found the legendary Northwest Passage. At the height of the fur trade, more than one hundred tons of trade goods were carried over the trail each year. The route became so important that the French built forts at each end of the passage to defend it.

One morning in June I set out along the trail, following the path into the cool, green woods, toward a spring hole that gave up brook trout. Like all portage trails the track was no wider than my boots, packed smooth and hard by centuries of constant use. Cushioned with brown pine needles, the trail rolled over hills, between hummocks, and around boulders and rocks. Although I was carrying nothing but the clothes on my back, I soon stopped to take a break beneath an enormous red pine. The tree had been a sapling when John Sayer, a partner in the Northwest Fur Company, walked the trail in 1804, enroute to company posts in the St. Croix country. After making the portage, his journal hints at the hardships and dangers regularly experienced by his men:

> Lake St. Croix Saturday 15th Sept 1804. At 6 A.M. Embark'd under heavy rain. Arrived at Noon at Namaiocawagun, the place where La Prairie pass'd the summer. I found

him & Seraphin with 2 men here. They had no provisions having left all their Oats [wild rice] in Cache. La Prairie made only 4 Small packs during the Summer. The Goods I had forwarded by Mr. La Mare was in Excellent condition. Mr. Reaume has been absent 20 days trading provisions at Paguegamant. We apprehend some Accident has befallen him.

What was it that lured voyageurs away from civilization to risk their lives in the northern wilderness? Sudden death, incapacitating injuries, starvation, and even cannibalism among their own ranks were taken in stride as they pushed their way west and northwestward across the continent. What reward did they hope to find? What prize did they seek? But then the trail led down a ridge and through the trees I caught a hint of blue as sunlight played on the Brule River. Instantly I was filled with the excitement men have always known when venturing toward the undiscovered and new. Although the country had been altered, the portage trail was still intact, and the river was as wild and changeless as ever. It made no difference how many men had visited that secret place: that day I believed I was the first to see the Brule.

It was the same feeling I'd had while searching for Cadotte's old post along the Namekagon. In 1784 Michel Cadotte, a trader on Lake Superior's Madeline Island, left his home there to build a post at the north end of the Namekagon-Court Oreilles portage in an attempt to control the trade at that point. Traces of the old trail are still visible in the woods south of Hayward, Wisconsin—the Mecca of muskie fishing.

The 2-1/2-mile-long portage links the Namekagon and Chippewa Rivers, and is best known for the part it played in the adventures of Jonathan Carver, the English explorer. Leaving

Prairie du Chien on the Mississippi in 1766, Carver's Chippewa guides warned him not to ascend that river; hostile Sioux controlled the upper Mississippi, and Carver's small party would have made easy prey. Instead, his guides led Carver up the Chippewa River to the Chippewa and Ottawa villages at Lac Court Oreilles; there they portaged into the Namekagon, paddling to the St. Croix and then ascending that stream to the Brule River passage. Eventually Carver wrote a popular book about his trip. The result was the first flood of European immigrants to America.

Once, while canoeing the Namekagon near the site of Cadotte's old post, I made contact with that distant past. I was catching smallmouths and searching for clues to pinpoint the post's exact location, and found it—suddenly and unexpectedly—along the riverbank. The banks were green and teeming with June's lush growth, but at one point near the waterline lay a band of bright, gold flowers, in sharp contrast against the emerald woods. I paddled toward the bank for a closer look and realized with a start that these were *fleur-de-lis*—the golden irises of Bourbon France.

For hundreds of years the fleur-de-lis was the symbol of French royalty. I thought of the king's ensign—a white flag emblazoned with the golden fleur-de-lis—and the way those banners once rode the winds above French settlements from Montreal to Winnipeg, and as far south as New Orleans. This was the emblem of New France, an empire that encompassed a third of North America. But when it fell to the British in 1763, the landscape was soon rid of all traces of the Bourbon dynasty. Today, a few place names, portage trails, and the occassional patch of fleur-de-lis are all that remain of the dream that was New France.

French colonists carried the plants to the New World with them and planted the flowers at their new homes, tokens of their ties to French kings and French soil. Even after the collapse of New France, when French Canadians like Michel Cadotte were pressed into the service of British fur trading companies, French voyageurs continued to plant fleur-de-lis at wilderness outposts, perhaps in memory of the glory they had lived and lost. On the day I discovered them along the Namekagon, all traces of Cadotte's old post were long gone. But in the golden bloom of fleur-de-lis it seemed as if he and his voyageurs had passed this way only yesterday.

In that moment the Old North came to life for me, and when I looked back on the Namekagon I could almost see the brigades of voyageurs moving along the stream in birch bark canoes, vermillion-tipped paddles blazing in the sun. I could almost hear the excitement in their shouts as they reached the bank and strode into the post before shouldering their packs to cross the portage toward a new horizon. Although the old post was gone the fleur-de-lis were still there; fishing was the portage trail between me and the past. I was tempted to pluck a flower and hold time in my hand, but in the end I decided it was best to leave them as they were, standing watch over the Namekagon and on all who passed that way.

Voyageurs measured the length of a portage in *poses*—one *pose* being the distance that trade goods could be carried before being set down. A *pose* served as both a resting place and as a kind of depot: all packs were brought to the first *pose* before any gear was moved to the next, a precaution against raids by Indians or rival traders. Most portages were two *poses* in length; however, the longest portage in all the North lay in Wisconsin, consisting of one hundred twenty poses—or forty-five miles! This was the old Flambeau Trail that led from the waterfall-studded canyon of Lake Superior's Montreal River to the placid lakes and streams of Wisconsin's Lac du Flambeau region.

Although much of this trail has been buried under reservoirs and roads, traces of it are still visible near Long Lake, a favorite resting place of voyageurs. Not long ago I was walking a narrow footpath that led toward the lake, wondering if it might not be a part of the Flambeau Trail. From accounts I had read in old journals from the fur trade, I was sure I was on the right track; yet, like any explorer, there was no way to know for sure until I reached the end. At one point the trail crossed a little creek and I stopped to rest, thinking I'd make a little *pose* of my own. I sat back against the trunk of a giant white pine, laid my fishing gear aside, and kicked my heels into the earth. Just below the duff I struck something brittle.

When I picked up the object and brushed away the dirt, I found the fragment of an old clay pipe. It was badly discolored and weathered by the years, but there was no mistaking its origin. From past fishing trips I knew it was similar to clay pipes found in archaeological digs for voyageur artifacts along Minnesota's Grand Portage. Perhaps it was left behind by a voyageur who had paused for a smoke on his way down the Flambeau Trail.

A pause at that place seemed a natural thing to do, and though the voyageur and I were worlds apart in time, a simple human impulse remained changeless. I held the clay shard in my hand and tried to imagine its story, as well as the man who had left it there long ago. I would never know that country as the voyageur had known it, but because of the portage trail I had learned something of its magic and its past. I listened closely, hoping to hear its echo in the wind, but there was only the rustling of pine boughs, the gurgling creek, and the sense of being caught up in something timeless and transcendent. This is the lure of portage trails, and the real meaning of wilderness everywhere.

Every portage trail is a little adventure. Along the way we escape modern life, make contact with the past, and are free to press on toward new horizons of our own. There, for a little while, we can be explorers, and search for an end that cannot be known.

TWELVE

Castle Creek

She stood there with her hand-me-down spincasting rod, dirty and disheveled after digging for worms. She was ten years old and could have passed for a boy, except for the pigtails beneath her baseball cap. Her name was Rachel and she was my niece.

"Can we go fishing today?" she asked.

I looked across the kitchen table at my sister. It was June and the two of them had come up to my cabin for a week's vacation. They'd arrived the night before on two flat tires, and from the start Rachel had steered every conversation toward fishing. She had seldom been outside of a city, and like a lot of kids from single-parent families, the closest she had ever come to fishing was just dreaming about it. She talked about her fantasies as though they were real. It was a while before I realized that much of her young life was probably imaginary.

"I told Rachel you might take her if you weren't busy," my sister said. "Maybe you could show her Castle Creek."

"Castle Creek," Rachel repeated. "My mom's told me all about it. That's where you used to take her when she was a kid. Brook trout, mostly. And all the big ones are in Sanderson's Hole."

"You sound like you know it," I said.

"She does," said my sister. "Some kids ask for fairy tales at bedtime. With Rachel, it's fishing stories."

"Please, can we go?" Rachel asked. "I dug the worms."

My heart wasn't in it. I hadn't fished Castle Creek in almost twenty years: it was a place where any kid could usually take a limit of diminutive brook trout, but a grown man would never waste his time with it. Narrow, brushy, and often too small to make a cast, it was where I'd taken Rachel's mom to fish when she was still a girl.

I moved to the North to attend college, but that was only an excuse to be near good fishing. Within weeks I fell in with fishing guides, backwoodsmen, and other riffraff; soon I dropped out of school and took up life in the woods. I was also in love with a fisherman's daughter who took a chance and married a fishing bum. In those days, I worked just enough odd jobs to bankroll my next fishing trip; later still, I'd write an occasional fishing story for outdoor magazines whenever unexpected expenses—like having babies—turned up.

Together we built a cabin at a remote and abandoned logging camp that just happened to sit on one of the best trout streams in Wisconsin. Our home soon became a fishing camp for relatives, and there were plenty of those—I'm the oldest of seven kids, and each of them would take turns visiting. My sister, Carm—Rachel's mother—visited us the most and always stayed the longest, helping out with our infant son. When she wasn't washing diapers or chauffeuring Peg the eighty miles to Nick's pediatrician, Carm and I would pass a good chunk of summer by fishing Castle Creek and sharing dreams. Now, years later, she was visiting me with a child of her own.

"Please," Rachel begged, in that whiny way that kids have. "Please, Uncle Jack. Can we go fishing? *Please*?"

An hour later my truck was parked at the end of a logging road, and we were bucking hazelbrush along the trail to Castle Creek. Rachel and I walked the old trail exactly as I used to with her mother: crawling under windfalls, bulldozing through brush, swatting at black flies and mosquitoes every inch of the way. Good Lord, I thought, why am I doing this? Then, through an opening framed by silver birches, I caught a glint of sunlight on the shining waters of Castle Creek.

The brook was much smaller than I recalled. Now there were places I could leap, and enormous boulders that had once loomed like mountains were simply large, lichen-crusted rocks. But the amber-colored pools were as deep as ever, and the water was still as dark and clear as an icy Manhattan.

I could only guess at the number of times I'd dropped a line into Castle Creek. Hundreds, certainly; perhaps more. To be sure, there was a time when the stream was as familiar to me as my own reflection. But now no sense of intimacy remained. I had hoped that a place like Castle Creek would be changeless, but trout streams change as much as the people who fish them. Only the love of such places is ageless.

We worked our way downstream, Rachel casting at every little lie that could possibly hold a trout, behind mossy logs and black boulders, in the bright and transparent water near the banks, and in the cool, long-shadowed places where the boggy earth quaked beneath our sneakers.

At the place where my sister always liked to fish, I impaled another worm on a trout hook for Rachel. The glassy eddy was much as I remembered, right down to the stack of beaver slash that always formed a little dam above it. Dark water gurgled over the slash. Floating twigs and bits of duff swirled back into the eddy.

"Toss your worm to the head of the pool, up there," I told Rachel.

She made a little cast and we watched as the pink worm drifted in the amber current, twirling with the floating twigs and duff before being pulled under. The line tightened and the tip of her rod suddenly twitched, rather feebly.

"You've got one," I said.

She yanked back wildly as a six-inch brookie came hurtling out of the water and onto the bank.

"I got one! I got one!" She threw the rod down and clapped her hands. "He's beautiful, isn't he, Uncle Jack? More beautiful than I imagined."

"Yes, he is," I said.

The fish was brightly speckled with luminous grays and greens, and flecked with scarlet spots along its flanks. I'd almost forgotten how beautiful the wild trout of Castle Creek could be. I held up the fish for Rachel to admire.

"Can we keep him?" She squatted beside me as I washed the fish free of dirt. At six inches, the brookie was just legal. But it was her first fish. What the heck, I thought.

I showed her a patch of ostrich ferns and together we picked a wad. We rinsed the leaves of dust and dirt, wrapped the fish in them, and dropped it into the canvas creel. I slung the creel over her shoulder and she gave a hoot. "Oh! I can feel him moving in there!" she squealed. "This is so *cool!*"

We took three more fish, as tiny as the first, before reaching Sanderson's Hole. The deepest, widest spot on the stream, its fish were the largest on Castle Creek. It was late afternoon and in the waning light the water was as dark as teak. The high bank was soft and spongy with spruce needles; a blue cluster of forget-me-not lay beside the stream. Rachel climbed down the bank and picked a handful of the wildflowers. "For mom," she said. Then she asked me to hold the flowers so she could make a cast.

In an instant she was on to a fish. I saw the brook trout's flaming flanks as it turned in the water. The line sliced the surface as the fish raced for the bottom. But something went wrong and the reel's drag began to whine. The line was taut and the rod tip quivered, but Rachel wasn't retrieving any line.

"He must be a big one," she said.

"I think you're snagged, Rach. Here, let me see." I took the rod and could feel the fish still tugging at the other end, twenty feet away, but the monofilament was tangled around some underwater obstruction. There was nothing to do but snap the line and lose the fish. I looked at Rachel, on her hands and knees at the edge of the bank, peering down into the creek. "My fish is stuck," she said—it was almost a cry. Then she looked at me and brightened. "You can help him, can't you, Uncle Jack?"

"I can cut the line and let him go," I said.

"But this is Sanderson's Hole." Her voice was desperate. "He might be a big one. I *know* he's a big one."

But there wasn't much chance of that. On Castle Creek the largest trout were barely eight inches.

"Please," Rachel begged.

I looked at the ten-year-old girl at my feet, and saw her mother—my sister—as I always remembered her: as a young girl fishing the untroubled waters of Castle Creek on a long-gone summer's day, when her world was still untried and new, and she was unaware that dreams can break your heart.

A line from Robert Browning came to mind: "A brother's love exceeds All the world's loves in its unworldliness." Love seeks not limits but outlets.

I gave Rachel the rod and then slid down the bank into water as deep as my waist. It was icy cold, and as soon as I was in, I regretted my decision to be gallant. I grabbed the line with one hand and waded out into the hole, as the chilly, brandy-colored water crept above my chest. Once I stumbled over a sunken log and almost went under; I would have given up, if Rachel hadn't been on the bank cheering me on. The water climbed up to my shoulders; I was almost floating by the time I found where the line had wrapped itself around a submerged branch. I reached under the surface, feeling my way along the slimy limb to the knot, and snapped the branch with my thumb. The line was free and I shouted for Rachel to reel in. Then I turned and waded back to join her.

"I knew he'd be a big one," she said. She was on her knees, holding the trout with both hands. It was really a small fish—a little larger than the others—but for Rachel it was the perfect ending to a story which, until that moment, she had lived only in her dreams. I had never seen her look happier, and I had never felt more like a damsel's champion.

"Thank you," she said.

I helped her look for ostrich ferns, and then together we carefully cleaned, washed and wrapped the trout. As we did, Rachel held up each fish to the light, admiring the brookies as if they were jewels. Then we put the trout back into the creel and turned toward home.

We walked slowly, a tiny girl of ten and a middle-aged duffer—a maiden and her soggy knight-errant—talking of family, brook trout, and Castle Creek, and of the love we sometimes mistake for fishing.

THIRTEEN

Little Victories

It may be the feistiest fish in the North, yet the rock bass is a fish without a following. Despite feeding habits that are more voracious than other fish and an unequalled willingness to strike, the rock bass lacks the mystique of muskies, the magic of trout, and the prestige of walleyes, pike, and largemouths. Instead, rock bass are thought of as a "freebie"—it's fine if you catch one, but if you don't catch any, that's all right, too.

My own fondness for rock bass was a long time in coming. Like most kids who grow up in Wisconsin, I'd thought of rock bass as annoying, bait-stealing runts that I'd sometimes catch while fishing for smallmouths. But now—much older and, hopefully, a little wiser—I know it's the little victories that count.

My affection for rock bass began during a trip to the Quetico-Superior country. We had come a long way up the rocky north shore of Lake Superior before turning inland over the Sawbill Trail. After months of planning, we were finally setting out on a week-long fishing trip through Minnesota's canoe country, and we were filled with expectations of things to come. But as luck would have it, the smallmouths weren't biting, the walleyes were tight-lipped, and the few pike we took were as thin as ribbons.

A stiff, steady east wind was the culprit. Foam-specked combers marched across the lakes, pinning us to shore. When we did venture out, the fishing was nonexistent. By midweek I think both of us were feeling disappointed.

One morning my partner and I shoved off for a group of islands that loomed like galleons in the distance. The wind was full of bluster, the lake was in a champagne mood, and we bucked spumes and spray all the way to the lee of the islands. Given the breezy conditions, it was not the best place to cast a line: any feeding fish would be lying off windward shores but our canoe was no match for the whitecaps. Instead, we tossed crankbaits with little enthusiasm toward the rocks of a submerged and sheltered point where we suspected the eel grass might be hiding a few walleyes. On the third or fourth cast, something hit my Rapala with a shock.

"Got one!" I gave a shout, sure that I had tied into a nice walleye. I felt ridiculous when the fish finally surfaced: it was a chunky rock bass, no bigger than my hand.

My friend was about to make some snide remark when suddenly he gave a hoot. In an instant he was into it, battling a rock bass that fought like a smallmouth—up to the surface and out, back into the weeds, and around the canoe.

"I think our luck just changed," my friend said. He admired his catch—a dark, red-eyed, half-pound rock bass, flecked with gold along its flanks.

The fish had no trouble inhaling our plugs, and when we switched to tiny spoons and spinners, we took rock bass on what seemed to be every cast. We later learned that other anglers in the area were being skunked, and for many that week in the Boundary Waters would be a disappointment. But for the rest of our trip, rock bass provided meals and hours of fast-paced fun, as well as the sense of having faced a challenge and won.

Since then, I often fish for rock bass, usually when other fish are "off the bite." Highly aggressive with an eclectic appetite and an enormous mouth when compared to its size, rock bass will usually take a hook under any conditions. But this readiness to strike doesn't mean a catch of rock bass is a sure thing: indiscriminate in feeding habits, they are very finicky about habitat. This is another reason why rock bass lack the wide appeal of other fish: most anglers don't know where to find them. Instead, they think of rock bass as a fluke—you may catch one, but you'll never catch enough to make a meal.

Like walleyes, rock bass shun direct sunlight and are always found near weeds and rocks. On lakes, stony shorelines studded with boulders, overhanging trees, and reeds will usually conceal rock bass, as do gravel bars that crest near enough to the surface to produce vegetation and shade. While the fish will take any kind of lure throughout the year, tiny jigs often work best.

One year, just after the ice went out, I was fishing with friends on Lac Vieux Desert, that big lake that straddles the Wisconsin-Upper Michigan border. The land was in flood and the country's stark solitudes still had the gray look of winter. Earlier I had bragged about the lake's spring fishing; now I was the butt of everyone's jokes. We were fishing for crappies in water as cold as ice cubes, but if the fish were there, they refused to strike. By noon the others agreed that it was hopeless and went back to the cabin, empty-handed and numb. Rather than endure their jeers and jibes, I decided to stay out on the lake and fish.

I kept close to shore with the wind at my back, tossing a marabou crappie jig at the sunny side of boulders, letting the jig sink into the shadows before "swimming" it back on a tight line over the bottom's rubble. At one spot the wind had piled up driftwood against the rocks; the limbs of submerged trees pierced the surface like gnarled fingers. I swam the jig past the edge of the flotsam. Almost immediately there was a strike.

On the light rod the rock bass was as scrappy as a brook trout. Soon I had a half-dozen fish, all of a size just right for the pan. At the cabin, my friends stared at my catch in disbelief. For once I was the center of attention, and I felt as though I had won a little victory.

Even a first-time fisherman can usually catch enough rock bass to look like an accomplished angler. This is especially important when fishing with kids; their enthusiasm notwithstanding, youngsters soon grow bored with fishing unless they catch something. Because of this, rock bass make an ideal quarry when a child is first learning angling skills.

When my son Nick first picked up a spinning rod, I thought I'd given him a weapon. His casting technique could clear any stream of other anglers; on lakes, he snagged every rock and tree. He was probably too young but he insisted on learning, hurling jigs and spinners and crankbaits without results. Slowly, his interest began to dissipate. He was almost ready to admit defeat when I suggested we fish for rock bass.

It was mid-July, summer was lush, and rock bass would be feeding at the surface in the evening. I reasoned that with a popper Nick might at least get a few strikes and not snag bottom as he did with other lures.

We arrived at the lake late in the day, just as twilight struck. Darkening shorelines trembled with loon calls. On a distant ridge, the sunset was a quivering red ball. The looking-glass lake brimmed with quiet tension, its surface reflecting the clouds.

We pushed off in the canoe, and I took the stern and paddle while Nick sat with his spinning rod in the bow. We were characters in a dream, gliding past boulder-strewn shorelines where tall pines stood in soundless colonnades. I tied a popper to the line and Nick began casting to the shadows, towards the masts of fallen timbers, and the darker water over rocks. The air whined with the steady buzz of insects. Suddenly, near a boulder, a splash broke the quiet spell.

For once the line unfurled without a hitch as Nick dropped the popper near the sound. At first the lure just sat there, riding its own ripples before Nick twitched the rod. Then there was a swirl as the limber rod bent.

"I've got him!" Nick shouted.

The size of the rock bass surprised even me when it broke water. It dashed to the bottom and darted for the rocks, but when it came close, the net was ready. I slipped the net under the biggest rock bass I had seen in some time: twelve inches long and all of a pound. Its brassy, spotted flanks glistened beautifully in the last rays of sunlight. We sat there saying nothing, just looking at that fish while shorelines echoed with trembling loon calls.

"He's a beauty, isn't he, Dad?" Nick asked.

"You bet," I told him. "He's bigger than any rock bass I ever caught."

Nick's face was aglow and in his eyes was the satisfaction that comes only once in the life of a boy, when he has done what he once believed was impossible, and has accomplished it better than anyone else. I also knew that in the years ahead, whenever Nick thought of the places he had been or the things he used to do, he would remember that night on the looking-glass lake, when loon calls echoed with trembling deception, and he learned that nothing is more illusory than defeat.

To be sure, the lowly rock bass has few admirers. It lacks glamour and prestige, and it isn't difficult to catch. But for me, a stringer of rock bass means as much as a trophy pike or trout. Big fish may add spice to life, but it's the little victories that mean the most.

FOURTEEN

The Land That Time Forgot

The French have a term for it: *à la mémoire*. It means to experience something from out of the past; to recall a time or place of long ago. And it's a phrase that often comes to mind when traveling the Headwaters-Sylvania country.

The Headwaters sits atop the Great Divide, that height of land that separates Wisconsin and Upper Michigan, and the two principal drainage areas of the upper Midwest. A green and rugged wilderness, the land literally shimmers with a thousand lakes and streams. In the beginning, the fishing attracts most people here, but after a while something else exerts its pull: for this is land that time forgot, where the past still lingers like an echo.

As recently as 1966, much of it had never been visited except by Indians and a handful of white men. Even now there are lakes on both sides of the state border holding fish that have never seen a boat or canoe. And in the Sylvania tract itself, no less an authority than the U.S. Forest Service claims that the country remains exactly as the French found it three hundred years ago.

Since then, birch bark canoes of early explorers have given way to Kevlar and aluminum, but the canoe remains a favorite means of travel here. In all the world, only three other areas are comparable to the Headwaters in terms of water density per square mile of land—southern Finland, east of the Bothnia Gulf, the Quetico-Superior country of Ontario-Minnesota, and the St. Croix watershed where my cabin sits. In fact, 40 percent of the Headwaters' surface *is* water. Admittedly, the wilderness character of some waterways has been spoiled by development and commercialism. But once away from the busy resort towns and popular fishing lakes, the only company likely to be encountered will be bald eagles and loons.

Hidden Lake is a good example. I call it that because, like many of the small bass lakes that dapple the area, it's an anonymous, conifer-rimmed pool of rain-pure water that appears on few maps.

My wife, Peg, and I came across it by accident in early May. We were far to the southeast of Lac Vieux Desert, the source of the Wisconsin River, traveling the "lost lakes" region of the Nicolet National Forest. The ice had gone out of big lakes like Kentuck and Franklin only two weeks before, and a guide we met told us to forget fishing these places until the weather warmed. Instead, he suggested we try some of the smaller lakes hidden away in the forest—places like Quartz, Luna, and White Deer. He claimed these little lakes warmed up quickly after the thaw, and would usually produce fish. Almost nobody visited remote lakes like Imogene and Whispering, he said: the only way in to them was over brushy logging trails, making them inaccessible to fishermen with hi-tech, trailer-toted boats.

We took the guide's advice and headed north on Old Military Road, east of Eagle River. The narrow road often led through tunnels of white pines, the boughs of the big trees entwined overhead. The road had once been an Indian trail, and was later used as a defense route by pioneers, linking the frontier of northeastern Wisconsin with Fort Wilkins in Upper Michigan. Much of the road is blacktop now, but where it hooks to the west near the

Deerskin River, the original trail still runs due north, lying like a scar in the forest. It was here where we switched to the old furrow, the trail grown up in popple and balsam brush, before veering off on another trail that weaved like a rollercoaster around tamarack swamps and over glacial ridges, before abruptly halting at a solid wall of big, white pines. Beyond the trees, glistening in the sunlight, lay Hidden Lake.

"What do you think?" I asked Peg.

"It's remote, all right," she said. "It doesn't look like anyone has been back here in years."

The likelihood of that was slim, but Hidden Lake had that sort of feeling. We pitched camp, gathered wood, and by the time I slipped the canoe into the water, the country was teeming with twilight.

Loons were calling across the lake, the water flat as a mirror. I paddled into the nearest bay, where the limbs of submerged trees poked through the surface like masts of lost ships. In the gloaming, the dark, magenta sky was as red as a moccasin-flower: mallards passed against the sunset. I tied a lure to the end of my line and tossed the plastic minnow toward shore.

The calm erupted as a big largemouth hit the bait. The bass jumped and leaped and splashed and flipped; I was shocked by its size. Later, when I put the tape to it, the fish measured twenty-two inches and the scale sagged at an even seven pounds. I handled the bass with wet hands, careful not to damage its protective mucus shield, holding it by the lip as I fumbled with my free hand for a cigarette to calm myself.

From the bow of the canoe, Peg snapped away with her camera. "You're not going to keep him, are you?" she asked.

Not going to keep him? Are you crazy? I thought. It was the kind of trophy I'd always dreamed about catching: a big, wild fish from a wild place, as pure and unsullied as the first dawn.

But Peg was right. The spell of that country had taken hold of me, too: I couldn't keep that fish anymore than I could carve my initials into one of the great pines that stood guard over the lake. The bass was too large, too beautiful to keep—too much a part of that wild and primitive country to end up lacquered and lifeless on a wall.

I held the fish in the water, waiting to make sure it wasn't injured or fatigued, gently forcing water to circulate through its gills. In time, the bass darted away.

"You can always come back here and maybe catch him again," Peg said.

"Sure," I told her, and I believed it, too.

But although I've tried to get back to Hidden Lake many times since then, I've never been able to find the trail that leads there. Like others who have discovered the lost lakes of the Headwaters region—only to never find them again—the entire experience has taken on the ambience of a dream, as though it were only a story I once heard about long ago, and which exists only as a secondhand memory—an *à la mémoire* of which I couldn't possibly be a part.

And yet, whenever I begin to doubt, I look at a photograph above my desk. In the picture the red sky is the color of moccasin-flowers, and I can almost hear the loons. The twilight is teeming with mystery and magic, and I'm in a canoe on a wilderness lake, holding the biggest bass I've ever caught in the North.

*　　　*　　　*

The Headwaters area has no legal boundaries. Geographically, it lies between the Flambeau Flowage on the west and the "lost lakes" region of the Nicolet Forest in the east. From the resort town of Minocqua, Wisconsin, and the Chippewa lands at Lac du Flambeau, the Headwaters' lakes sweep away to the northeast, following the retreat of ancient glaciers as far north as Bond Falls in Upper Michigan. In Wisconsin, the Nicolet and the state's Northern Highland Forest form part of the area; in Michigan, the Ottawa National Forest takes over. Together, it adds up to a wild area twice the size of Rhode Island.

But it's at night, after the canoe is pulled up on shore and the campfire burns like the beacon of a safe harbor, that the real lure of the country begins to emerge from dark shadows. It begins with the trembling cry of a loon, the hoot of an owl, or the frenzied yapping of brush wolves. Things begin to crack and snap beyond the ring of the campfire's light, and in the place where you had gone to fetch water only moments before, the heavy thud of fur-padded footfalls begin to stalk the shore.

You build up the fire but its light is little comfort. Common sense tells you the sounds are only raccoons and rabbits, and yet something else tells you that common sense sometimes lies. There's a presence all around you, shapeless and without substance, but nevertheless a presence that is very much alive.

I felt it one night among the bogs east of Star Lake. Earlier that day I had found the place where a band of Potawatomis had made their last stand against the onslaught of late-nineteenth-century loggers. Shadows of a camp were still clearly etched among the trees; mounds of earth encircling perfectly square depressions marked where soil had once been banked against the sill logs of cabins. Carefully digging through the duff, I slowly uncovered the years, unearthing a pile of old pine knots that someone had stacked in the distant past, the knots still sound after a hundred years.

That night, paddling along the heather of a bog, I had the uneasy feeling that I was not as alone as I thought. A stack of old pine knots had put me in touch with past lives, and I could feel the presence of phantoms in the mists that swirled about the lake, engulfing my canoe and shrouding the shores. It felt as if I had left the world behind, transported to a place beyond the common and easily perceived. Suddenly I was no longer a modern man out on a weekend camping trip, but part of a wild and haunted land.

*   *   *

That sense of the surreal only deepens as you move north into Upper Michigan's Sylvania tract. Here, among its virgin hardwoods and hemlocks, are places where people seldom wander.

The country was first explored by white men during the fur trade, and as late as 1890 it was still largely the domain of Indians. Then, in 1900, officials of the United States Steel Corporation purchased 21,000 acres of timber east of Thousand Island Lake for a private sporting reserve. They dubbed it "Sylvania," named for their lodge on Thousand Island Lake. To insure that the area remain inaccessible to all others, the boundaries were posted and armed guards were hired to patrol its perimeter. In this way, the Sylvania escaped the encroachment of the twentieth century.

In 1940, much of the Sylvania was purchased by L. P. Fisher of the Fisher Auto Body Company: like his predecessors, he preserved its virgin quality by denying the public access. It wasn't until his death, when the property passed on to his heirs, that the Sylvania finally became part of the surrounding Ottawa National Forest. In 1966, the U.S. Forest Service purchased it from Fisher's estate for $5,740,000.

The area today remains as pristine a wilderness as ever. Timber wolves are occasionally sighted, as well as the once thought-to-be-extinct eastern cougar. Because all water flows away from the Headwaters in four directions—southwest to the Mississippi, south and southeast to Lake Michigan, and north to Lake Superior—the Sylvania's lakes have no inlets to supply nutrient matter. The result is ice water-clear lakes whose chemical composition is that of rain. Due to this and their previous inaccessibility, the lakes contain a virgin fishery, unchanged from the time when Indians speared walleyes here from birch bark canoes.

Although the fish of Sylvania's lakes are very large, they are also very old; and while anglers are allowed to keep some fish, its bass, northerns, trout, and walleyes are too great a prize to be taken as just another trophy. Like the rainbow bridges that span its woods after a summer storm, the Sylvania—and its fish—belong to another realm. They are something to marvel over, look at, and then release, rather than to capture and keep.

But the temptation to take fish is great. Once, at Clark Lake, I spooked two largemouths that looked as big as salmon. And at Deer Island and Loon Lakes there are smallmouth bass that are larger than any bronzebacks caught in the North in the last fifty years. But this virgin fishery is part of what makes the Headwaters-Sylvania area a special place—a place where our wilderness heritage remains alive and intact.

One experience I had in the Sylvania remains especially clear and real to me, an *à la mémoire* I often recall, whenever the hunger for lonely places returns. It was October and the snow was flying. I was making the last canoe trip of the season, and just before dark I came across a large beaver flowage already rimmed with ice. At the far end was the largest beaver dam I have ever seen—eight feet high and as long as a football field—and as I climbed up on it to look out over the lake, a flock of blue geese came in low over the dam, filling the wintery woods with their heartbreak cries.

The dam was ancient—far older than any living man—and it made me think about all those who had come there before me, on foot or in canoes, to trap fur, gather rice, catch fish, and to answer the call of wilderness. For an instant I was made aware that, there—in that country—I was only the latest link in an unbroken chain of existence that spanned the centuries, a way of life that reached back into the days of the voyageurs, the Indians, and beyond. I looked down at my canoe and then out across the country, and there it was—*à la mémoire*—an experience of things past; but there, on that beaver flowage, the past was quite near, no farther away than the portage trail around the dam.

There is such a thing as transcendence, and man's perennial longing to escape his life's confines. I once found both on a beaver dam in the wilderness, in a land forgotten by time.

FIFTEEN

Fare Game

I'm always a little amused at the menus described in outfitters' advertising brochures. For example, I'm planning a wilderness canoe trip this summer, and here's a sampling of the menu my outfitter has prepared for me:

Breakfast 2nd Day
Coffee or tea (brewed)
Orange juice (powdered)
Home-made applesauce
Tangy Western omelette
Hash browns
Canadian bacon
Fresh blueberry muffins (optional)

Come on now, who is he trying to kid? I've been on plenty of canoe trips, and if I ate like that I'd need to trade my canoe for a barge.

Oh, the outfitters live up to their part of the bargain all right. They deliver everything promised, and more. But nobody on any wilderness canoe trip that I've ever been part of has had the patience or inclination to prepare tangy Western omelettes first thing in the morning.

A typical breakfast menu from one of my wilderness excursions would read something like this:

Breakfast 5th Day
Coffee or Kool-Aid (instant)
Cigarette (if any are left)
Piece of hardtack (linoleum)
Air

I guess food just doesn't rate as a high priority with me when I'm on a wilderness fishing trip. Sure, I'd eat it if someone else took the time to prepare it, but most of the people I usually throw in with are just as anxious as I am to hit the water first thing in the morning. The last thing any of us want to do is to slave over a campfire preparing tangy Western omelettes while everyone else is out on the water catching fish. Besides, no one likes having to clean up the mess that goes along with making breakfast. If doing breakfast dishes was my idea of fun, I could have stayed at home and saved a couple of bucks.

Lunch is a different matter. I get a kick out of the pamphlets that lodges and resorts send to prospective customers, describing the classic "Northwoods shore lunch." To read them, you'd think a shore lunch was what the gods of Olympus dined on before nectar and ambrosia came along.

The brochures tell of things like "cheesy, au gratin potatoes, sweet Bermuda onions, hearty pan-fried bannock," and walleye fillets that they assume I will catch "fresh from an ice-cold lake, breaded, seasoned, and cooked to a delectable golden-brown. *Mmmmm.* You can almost taste it, can't you?"

I'm sorry, but I can't. I don't know why it is, but you can set me down on the finest walleye lake on the Canadian Shield and my presence will have the same effect on fishing as a double dose of rotenone.

I've been lugging around a cast-iron fry pan and a sack of potatoes for as long as I can remember, in the hope of one day lunching on "fresh-caught walleyes from an ice-cold lake." So far, the most elaborate shore lunch I've enjoyed has been a cigarette and a can of warm beer.

Fishermen place a great deal of emphasis on food, which is surprising because we eat so little of it while actually fishing. Opening weekend is a good example of that. I fish opening weekend with a half-dozen guys and every year we each kick $50 into a pot to buy food. That's $350 worth of food for seven men for three days of fishing. Ultimately, we buy $10 worth of food and $340 worth of taco dip and cheese puffs.

One foodstuff common to all anglers is the sandwich. Sandwiches are as much a part of outdoor life as fly rods and brook trout. Basically, sandwiches fall into two categories: the ones you make yourself and the ones that are made for you.

The ones you make for yourself usually consist of coarse rye bread, venison steak smothered in horseradish, topped by a thick slab of aged cheddar and a mound of sweet onions. They have the same heft and weight as a full box of goose loads. The sandwiches prepared for you by others—guides, wives, or teenage daughters—are quite another matter. These things usually consist of a dab of tacky peanut butter held in place by two pieces of dry bread that are indistinguishable from cedar shingles.

You can tell a lot about a man by the sandwiches he eats. Here in Wisconsin, real outdoorsmen favor "cannibal" sandwiches—raw ground sirloin dusted with an inch of cayenne pepper and topped with an onion so caustic it can make your nose bleed. These are the same guys who wade the icy, spring slush of Lake Superior to net smelt wearing nothing but Malone pants. No waders, no hip boots, no insulated clothing—just ratty wool pants and a pair of old hunting boots. At the other extreme is the fellow who packs a basket lunch of neat, little ladyfinger sandwiches, tiny tins of imported bergamot jam, and a steaming samovar of Earl Grey tea. Sometimes he'll pack a flask of peach brandy, too: if he does, somebody in Malone pants usually wrestles it away.

Another type of outdoorsman is the remote stream fisherman who always forgets and leaves his sandwiches back at the car. Being a friend, it's only natural that you'd want to share your lunch with him—unless he's well-known as a habitual moocher. This is the prevailing attitude among my own companions, whose lack of charity gives new meaning to the term "misanthrope." Due to their pettiness, I've had to survive many a day on distant streams without lunch. When the fish are biting, it sure beats making a two-mile walk back to the car.

SIXTEEN

Summer Dreams

Pike fishermen are different from other anglers. Unlike your typical, rednecked "bassin'" fanatic, pike men use "rods," not "sticks," and they never speak in tongues. Nor are they anything like your average trout enthusiast: to a pike fisherman a Red Ibis is a tropical bird. Walleye anglers sometimes come close, but no self-respecting pike fisherman would ever mount a thirty-inch fish. And maybe that's what sets pike fishermen apart: they're dreamers, and their dreams are *big*.

Something happens to a man when he sees a giant northern pike. A kind of fever addles his brain and a faraway look fills his eyes. It has to do with trusting tomorrow, and believing that even a larger fish lies somewhere upstream. I know, because I'm a pike fisherman. All too often I've followed that dream.

I can clearly recall the first time I came face to face with a twenty-pounder. It happened late one summer along a stream near Lake Michigan. The stream was the favorite place of small boys like myself who went there with willow-wand poles and a bucket of fathead minnows, hoping to catch a respectable northern. We fished below a culvert where the creek crossed a country road, and though the spindling pike we took were more like snakes than fish, each one was always a reason for joy and celebration.

We were warned to never venture upstream of the culvert. Beyond that lay a swamp, filled with quicksand and wild dogs that could easily run down a small boy and tear him limb from limb. Still, whenever I gazed upstream at the blue water and at the way the aspens reached out to form a canopy over the creek, I knew that sooner or later I would explore that forbidden place. Like a voice in a dream, it called me.

Finally the day came when I could resist the spell no longer. The land was brimming with the light and lushness of late summer. I walked upstream beneath the fluttering aspens like an explorer setting out in search of the unknown. Then the creek entered a dark and brooding swamp, and there I moved cautiously through the silent, sable gloom. When something suddenly cracked in the brush at my back, I was too frightened to look. Instead, I began running upstream, sure that I was racing toward doom.

But I never found the quicksand, or the wild dogs, or any of the horrors I had imagined. Instead, near the source of the stream, I found a deep pool of icy-clear water, rimmed with rocks and enormous cedar trees.

It was cool and quiet beneath the cedars—a hush far deeper than any I had known. The earth was cushioned with a mat of tawny needles, a gold carpet that caught the sun and dispelled the gloom. The unruffled, rocky pool was filled with small suckers: the low water of late summer had pulled them upstream to deeper holes. And then I saw it—a giant northern pike—and when I did I nearly gave a shout.

It was as big as a railroad tie, lying motionless in the reeds at the lip of the streambed depression. Its snout was pointed at the finning suckers, the big fish looking for all the world like a wolf poised to strike. It was the biggest pike I had ever seen—almost too big to be real. And when it suddenly swept down on the schooling suckers, I sensed that magic was at work.

I had walked in only a little more than a mile, yet the silence and isolation were complete. For the first time I was alone in a wild and primitive place, yet I felt completely at home. It was a place I wanted to know and explore, a place where—more than anywhere else—I felt I belonged. It was a lost fragment of a young world untouched by time, and the pike was my link to it. The fish was part of the distances I had traveled, part of the solitude and silence, part of the spell that had lured me upstream. It belonged to that little wilderness in a way I never could; yet I felt that if I could only catch it, I might also capture something of its world. That day I became a pike fisherman.

*   *   *

Nowadays, there are only two places to fish for giant northerns: ordinary places, and the Northwoods. Big pike are as much a part of the North as muskeg bogs and timber wolves. After all, what other fish goes by the name "northern"? Just the thought of big pike conjures images of spruce-rimmed lakes, whitewater rivers, and the quavering cries of loons beneath the Northern Lights. Fishermen who head north may catch smallmouths and walleyes, but secretly what we really want is the chance to take giant pike.

I've also found there are only two times to fish for big pike: ordinary times, and late summer. I look forward to pike fishing as summer ends because, as a teenager, it was the one time of year I could call my own. Most of my summer vacations were spent in doing odd jobs for spending money, and it wasn't until just before the start of school that I was free for some serious fishing.

When that time arrived, I would light out with a spinning rod and box of cheap spoons for the nearest stream that held both suckers and pike. As water levels dropped, the suckers moved upstream to cooler, deeper water. In turn, pike followed the fish and preyed on the run.

Back then, my usual partner was Dean. He was a year older than I was, so of course he knew everything. Dean claimed pike fishing was best when summer suckers were running. "You can go up streams no wider than a road, and find a dozen pike as big as fence posts lying in a run," he said. "You can pick and choose if you use artificials, throwing back anything less than ten pounds."

Once, during a Labor Day weekend, we pushed off in Dean's canoe and paddled across a flowage and up its tributary stream. The day was as hot as any of midsummer, but already the air carried a hint of change. Flocks of teal were moving south, and wild rice beds were ripe, ready to be beat and broken. May's fawns were sporting nubs: soon they'd be spiked-bucks and fair game.

*   *   *

The stream was relatively narrow with deep holes and long runs spread out between gravel riffles. It was the color of weak whiskey, but clear enough to reveal an abundance of schooling suckers. Once, close to the bank, we passed over what I thought was a sunken log; then came the swirl as the big northern turned in the water.

The next northern hit a hair-tail spinner Dean had tossed into the head of a deep run bordered by exposed boulders. Round and thick as cordwood, it was better than thirty inches.

"Nice fish," I told him.

"Yeah, but there's even bigger ones somewhere upstream."

Like all pike fishermen, Dean was a dreamer.

And we talked about our dreams. At the end of summer each of us would be leaving home to find out what lay beyond. We had no clear idea what we might find: we were only sure it would be something better than staying at home, placidly accepting lives we never made, or chose.

We beached the canoe and took two more fish from the run. Then there was a long lull and Dean grew restless. Finally he decided to strike out alone and search upstream for bigger fish. I stayed with the canoe, dreaming my own dreams of faraway places.

I can still see Dean wading upstream through a tunnel of balsam and pine, moving with the happy lilt of someone confidently advancing toward the far horizon of a dream. No matter what he found upstream, for Dean it would be an adventure.

A pike fisherman always has one eye fixed upstream. He's convinced that somewhere beyond the next bend lies the catch of his dreams. Others may ogle sixteen-inch brookies or an eight-pound bass, but a pike fisherman's quarry is so large that no body of water could possibly hold it. It's a dream as old as fishing itself. But to a pike fisherman it's a dream that matters.

*   *   *

Not long ago I went back to visit my parents' home near Lake Michigan. Once the house had sat at the edge of town, but now it was encircled by a city. I'd gone back to attend a funeral. After the wake, when everyone had left and I was alone with the past, I felt an inexplicable need to fish the river where I had spent so much time long ago. I wanted to catch one more northern pike from that river. Of course, not just any fish would do—this one would need to be the grandfather fish of all the North.

I took the pack rod and gear I keep in my car and wandered down to the river. The water was low, but in a deep depression downstream of a log jam I took a ten pounder on a wobbling spoon. A five-inch sucker was still in its gullet. Some things never change.

Not the town, though. It, its people, and my family had changed: times had changed, and perhaps, most of all, I had too. I had left as a boy, and now I had a son of my own. In the intervening years I had learned much about dreaming.

On a whim, I walked back in to the cedar and rock-rimmed pool where I had seen that giant pike years ago. The ancient cedars had weathered time much better than I, and the silent rocks were as changeless as ever. The pool was still clear, deep, and cold to the touch, and filled with suckers holding steady along the current's edge. I almost expected the big northern to reappear, and though it didn't, I knew it was there. Big pike like that are *always* there. Somewhere.

It's that kind of thinking that makes a pike fisherman different, and sets him apart like an island in a stream. When summer ends, and rods and reels lie cased and forgotten, only the dreams remain.

SEVENTEEN

In Praise of Perch

The yellow perch gets little respect. Though perch fillets are more pricey than salmon—and, in my opinion, more tasty—most anglers think of perch as diminutive, bait-stealing runts.

This is unfair to the fish to whom I owe my very existence. To understand this, you need to understand Wisconsin.

Like much of the state's population, my grandparents immigrated to Wisconsin from Poland in the early 1900s. My mother's side of the family were classical musicians from Krakow. My dad's relatives owned a distillery in Włocławek. All of them settled on or near Jones Island, a sandy hump in the Milwaukee harbor entirely populated by taverns and Polish fishermen transplanted from the Baltic Sea.

The Kulpas, who often had trouble navigating on open water, had no problem finding their way to taverns: to finance their fondness for *piwo* and vodka, some of them worked as commercial perch fishermen on Lake Michigan (one branch of the family still operates a fishing fleet). My mom's family would go slumming on Friday nights by visiting Jones Island after the boats were in, to buy fresh perch and smoked chubs. It was over a perch dinner wrapped in newspaper that my dad proposed to my mom.

I grew up with a twelve-foot cane pole in my hands beside the fishermen of Jones Island, soaking hellgrammites and peeled crayfish tails for jumbo perch. This was more than just a pastime in a place as thoroughly Catholic as Wisconsin. This was back in the days of Latin and meatless Fridays, when lying about the size of your catch was technically a sin. In addition to Fridays, there was also Lent, Advent, and Ember Days, when fish was the only "meat" allowed on our table. Together with my Grandma Anna, there were ten of us at that table: to paraphase Norman Maclean, in our family there was no distinction between fishing, religion, and survival.

I was not alone in this. Nearly every tavern in Wisconsin held Friday night fish fries for us Catholics. For seventy-five cents you'd get three perch fillets, rye bread and butter, a cup of coleslaw, and a pound of oily french fries so unctuous they'd slide down your throat without having to chew them. A generation later, when the perch crashed in Lake Michigan, the taverns switched to cod. Even now, when Catholics are no longer required to abstain from meat on Fridays, you can't travel far in Wisconsin without finding a tavern hawking a Friday night fish fry. Today the price is $6.95, but the french fries are still unctuous.

As a kid, on Sundays, I'd attend the 5:00 A.M. fisherman's Mass at St. Stanislaus, along with my dad and uncles. The church sat on the mainland bluffs high above Jones Island, its towering twin steeples standing like sentinels over the wide and empty expanse of Lake Michigan. Perch fishermen built the steeples as a landmark to find their way home when storms swept their boats beyond sight of land. After Mass we'd go down to the island with our cane poles, a can of worms, and a bucket of Braumeister beer drawn fresh from the brewery on Cleveland

Avenue. "The church is God between four walls," goes a Polish proverb. But I was beginning to suspect God was also there wherever I was fishing.

*   *   *

The big schools of jumbo perch are gone now from Lake Michigan for reasons no one can explain. Like meatless Fridays, I suspect the fish are gone for good. And while the abundant perch of inland lakes are the very same fish, most caught by anglers are the size of hot dogs. As a result, few people fish for perch.

That's fine with me because I usually have the jumbo perch all to myself. Those old-time Baltic fishermen with whom I soaked hellgrammites were good for a whole lot more than Polish jokes. They knew things about catching perch that no else seems to know or remember. But then they had to—their livelihood depended on it.

Perch are related to walleyes and prefer the same sort of water—clear, deep lakes and rivers with mild currents. But these are not necessarily the best places in which to catch perch. Unlike walleyes, perch are hardy fish that can thrive in extremely shallow lakes susceptible to winterkill—in which species like bass and bluegills suffocate under the ice. After a winterkill takes place, a shallow lake can explode with big perch.

Recently, when floods inundated South Dakota, receding waters left the state pockmarked with shallow lakes—some of them flooded pastures. These waters were created by record amounts of run-off, and stocked by lakes and rivers that overflowed. While other species were lost to winterkill, the perch thrived: today, foot-long perch are typical catches.

I don't need to travel to South Dakota to catch jumbo perch. In my own area I watch for shallow bays cut off from lakes and rivers by receding water levels. These are easy to find in years of drought. Even better are drained reservoirs. Not far from my cabin the immense Minong Flowage was drained to repair the dam, leaving behind isolated pockets of water. Here, in these isolated "lakes," I caught jumbo perch until the flowage was flooded again.

Check with bait shops or the local fisheries manager to learn which lakes in your own area experience winterkill. Some states, like Wisconsin, offer booklets that categorize every lake by type, depth, size, and kinds of fish. While shallow, weedy lakes with soft bottoms produce the most perch, the biggest fish are found in lakes with moderate vegetation and sand, rock, or gravel bottoms.

Ultralight spinning gear is the choice of serious perch anglers today. The rod should be responsive enough to detect light-biting fish, and lithe enough to flex against the mad dash of jumbo perch. A five-foot graphite rod with a reel loaded with four-pound-test monofilament will handle any situation.

Perch—more than any other fish—are attracted to bright objects. Twist a four-inch strip of aluminum foil into a sort of bow tie around your line, a few inches above a perch hook. Clip it in place with split shot. Wrinkle the exposed flaps of the foil to create a multifaceted surface that reflects light in all directions. Not only will the wad of foil attract more perch, but it will entice the largest and most aggressive fish into striking.

Another method I learned on Jones Island is to remove the hooks from a shiny jigging spoon, such as a small Swedish Pimple or Doctor Spoon. Tie the lure to your line and add a foot of monofilament to the split ring at the bottom of the spoon. To the end of this line, tie a No. 4 short-shank hook with a minnow hooked through the back. Lower the spoon until it hits bottom, then reel in a foot of line. Jigging the lure up and down will attract more perch, and again, the most aggressive and largest fish will strike. Set the hook as soon as you feel the pick-up.

Timing is important as well. Unlike walleyes, perch do not see well in low-light conditions. Noon to dusk is prime time for catching perch.

Common wisdom claims that if you catch one perch, others are nearby—so stay with the school and continue to fish. Unfortunately, common wisdom is sometimes wrong.

While a school of perch may contain two hundred fish, all of the perch in that school will be roughly the same size. If you're catching tiny fish, pull up anchor and head for deeper water. Schools of small perch stay in shallow water throughout the year, but schools of large perch are always found in deeper water after the spawn.

By June, big perch in deep lakes head for open water, schooling near bottom in twenty to forty feet of water: in shallow lakes, the deepest hole may be ten feet. In either case, big perch will always be found near some sort of structure. Seek out sandbars, submerged points, flooded sand grass, old beaver huts, and swamped timber.

After locating a submerged point or a sparse weedline, troll or drift-fish the area to find a school of perch. Attach a barrel swivel to your line, pinch some split shot above that, and add thirty inches of line to the swivel's other ring. Tie on a No. 4 hook and run it under the chin and through the lips of a two-inch minnow. Fish the minnow from the bottom up, slowly. Perch tend to follow a moving bait before striking, but they are weak swimmers and will give up the chase if the bait moves too fast.

Anchor as soon as you catch a fish. Use the same rig, but now hook the minnow under the dorsal fin. If the first two or three perch you catch are small, move on to the next place. If the first perch you catch there is also small, move again. If you continue and can't find large fish, either the lake's perch population is out of balance or the water lacks proper habitat (thin weeds, sandy/gravel/rock bottoms). In any case, find another lake.

Perch nibble at worms, grubs, crayfish, hellgrammites, fish eyes, and grasshoppers. They tend to grab the end of a bait and quickly swim away—when you try to set the hook, you reel in a mangled grub or ragged piece of worm. Fishing with two-inch-long shiner minnows prevents this. When a perch strikes, it first mouths the bait. Then it moves away a short distance, stops, and turns the minnow around to swallow it. When you feel this pause in the line, set the hook. This tendency to mouth the bait is the reason for hooking a minnow under its dorsal fin when you're not trolling.

Occasionally, even large perch steal minnows from baited hooks. If this is a problem, gently pull the minnow away when you feel the first strike. When a perch perceives its meal is resisting, it will immediately swallow the bait.

*   *   *

One trick I learned on Jones Island has produced more big perch for me than any other. It is this: perch can be caught with jigs, spinners, flies, poppers, and spoons, but big perch are caught on multiple-hook rigs.

There are several reasons for this. Big perch prefer deep water and will always be lying within inches of the bottom, and multiple-hook rigs keep more bait down on the bottom for longer periods of time. This is important because a school of perch will seldom bite for more than fifteen minutes. During that time you want as many hooks as possible in the water. And while schools of small perch are quick to strike, large perch are reluctant to do so unless other perch in the area are feeding. A multiple-hook rig can stimulate a feeding frenzy and move perch into striking.

The simplest rig is made by tying a small loop twelve inches above the end of your line. To the loop, attach a four inch dropper of ordinary kite string to which you've tied a floating yellow jig. Attach a long-shank gold hook to the end of your monofilament: use a piece of split shot to clip a strip of aluminum foil four inches above the hook. Bait both hooks with minnows.

This rig can be fished with or without a float. Either way, the kite string dropper is less likely to snarl your monofilament. If you use a float, set the bobber stop so that the long-shank hook rides three inches off the bottom, and then reel in slowly, occasionally twitching your rod tip and then pausing, in the same way you'd fish a jig.

As soon as a fish strikes, set the hook—but leave the rig in the water to attract more perch. Other fish in the area will be attracted and may strike the remaining bait. After you land both fish, get your line back in the water as soon as possible—a big perch will probably strike as soon as your rig hits bottom.

*   *   *

It's late Friday afternoon as I write this—quitting time for me. Jones Island is gone and the Braumeister brewery was torn down years ago, but there's still plenty of Milwaukee beer in my fridge and a cold one is just what I need. Peg is out on the lake, catching our perch supper: my job will be to peel and fry potatoes. Being the traditionalist that I am, they'll be absolutely unctuous.

EIGHTEEN

Silence

I was camping beside a small pond in the Rainbow Lake Wilderness Area of northwestern Wisconsin. I had made the long hike in alone, pitched my tent by the light of a fire, and ate a cold meal of cheese and hardtack before turning in for the night. I was exhausted and sleep should have come easily, but chilly temperatures repeatedly roused me through the night. Just before sunrise I gave up all hope of slumber. I rolled out of my blankets and coaxed the campfire back to life.

The only sound as I worked was the soft sputtering of the fire. Gray mists moved like soundless wraiths among the trees. It was that quiet time before dawn when the earth still lies sleeping, before leaves begin to flutter and birds start to sing.

I poured a cup of coffee and walked down to the lakeshore. Not a rise or ripple marred the serene lake. I sat down at the end of an old, abandoned dock, the gray, weathered planks worn smooth as doeskin. I sat there, listening to the hush and trying to be aware, knowing that at such times thoughts and perceptions are most clear. Here, if anywhere, I understood what the writer Thomas Merton was hinting at when he wrote about his first trip through the Catskills—a trip that eventually led him to embrace the life of a Trappist monk. "Oh, America," he wrote, "how I began to love your country! What miles of silences God has made in you for contemplation! If only people realized what all your mountains and forests are really for!"

I sat on the dock, peering into the untroubled water, basking in the tranquility and sense of well-being that only silence can give.

Everyone needs such quiet moments, whether it be an afternoon walk through a peaceful park, or an evening spent at home alone with a book. But in towns and cities silence is fleeting. Only in wilderness is it possible to escape the din.

We dwell in a world of noise. Open a window—anytime, anywhere—and you'll hear the clamor. It's there in the roar of engines, the hum of compressors, the whir of appliances, and the peripatetic cellular telephone. Increasingly, even wild places are noisy with powerboats, jet skis, trail bikes, and ATVs. While some areas have banned motorized travel in an effort to preserve wilderness, no law exists to preserve silence itself. To be sure, many of our environmental laws are the result of ecological hypochondria: yet silence, which is truly endangered, remains unprotected.

Not long ago silence was still teeming in the American outdoors. Anyone old enough to remember when the local hardware store was also the tackle shop will remember. We were different people then, content with simple joys and pleasures. We went to the wild to do primitive things in a primitive way. As a result, the sounds we heard in the woods were natural in origin: the wind in the trees, the calling of birds, the buzz of insects, the patter of rain. But silence has eroded under a rising tide of technology.

Recently, during a canoe trip down the remote East Fork of the Chippewa River, I pitched a camp far from the nearest town or road. I was alone with the sound of the rushing stream and the soft calling of a whippoorwill. At dusk I caught dozens of small-mouths on spinners in the fast water at Cedar Rapids, as well as two walleyes that I kept for supper. Later, as darkness descended, I sat by the campfire, delighting in the hush and profound sense of isolation.

Suddenly I heard the *thump* of aluminum canoes in the rapids above me. A party had set out late in the day, overburdened and unprepared: now they were growing frantic in the gathering dusk. They asked if they could share my camp and I welcomed them, knowing from experience the hazards and unpleasantries of searching for a campsite in the dark. Yet, even before my guests pitched their tent, one of them pulled a portable tape player from a Duluth pack and cranked up the volume. In an instant the silence was shattered and the wilderness was gone.

We no longer recognize silence for what it is, what it does, or why it is necessary. We think of it as a pause in the din, instead of what was there before bedlam. Carlyle observed that "Silence is the element in which great things fashion themselves." Without silence there can be no dreaming; without dreams, there is no greatness.

Classical philosophers define evil as the loss of a good that should be there. If that's true, our lack of silence is sinister. It is one more symptom of a clouded and increasingly common consciousness that distains all that is beautiful and good—whether it be simple courtesy, a peaceful life, a happy marriage, the history of a great nation, or the glory of fine art, beautiful music, and natural landscapes.

Without silence there can be no interior life. Instead, existence becomes an obsession for immediate and personal gain. When that happens, people lose all sense of hope and belonging, and scorn what used to be called "the common good." This may explain our growing cynicism and disregard of others, and why (despite an ever-burgeoning population) the number of fishermen continues to decline—as do the ranks of active voters, volunteers, clergymen, stable families, lasting friendships, and honest politicians. The shrill insist that we've never been happier. But to paraphrase Emerson, what you are shouts so loudly that it's impossible to hear what you claim to be.

Without silence, peace is impossible. A psychologist I know claims that when he feels anxious, alone, or displaced, it's the want of silence that gives life to his fears. Yet, if he escapes to a quiet and sheltered trout brook for a few hours, he soon finds the peace to soothe his troubled psyche—*psyche*, the Greek word for "soul."

The silences of wild places are not yet gone, but they are vanishing, and if the last of their solitudes are ever broken, a great part of what makes us Americans will be lost. Europe has its grand cathedrals and the East its ancient temples, but in America it is in the silences of wild places where hearts are humbled and spirit soars.

PART THREE

AUTUMN

NINETEEN

Brigadoon

Autumn is the shortest season in the North. Almost before you know it was there, it is gone. Because of that, not a day of it should be lost or squandered.

In Wisconsin, the hunt for autumn begins when the red-wings stop trilling—overnight, the birds vanish. Now begins the waiting and watching as the advancing tide of autumn unfolds.

One year I found a hint of it just after Labor Day. I was standing on a one-lane bridge above the Brule River, watching the river flood with daylight. For the first time it was cool enough for a jacket, and there was a hush to the stream that hadn't been there before. The Brule was a different river from what it had been when its pools were populated with summer anglers. Now the trails along its banks lay undisturbed; its solitudes were vast and teeming.

I waded out into the pool above the bridge and tossed a spinner at the grassy sweepers. Color was draining from the stream-side trees: beneath them, the bracken ferns were already spotted with rust. A clump of staghorn sumac gleamed with lemon-yellow and blaze-orange. At the head of the pool a maple was entirely crimson: it burned like a torch.

A single, red leaf fluttered down from the tree. It landed like a feather on the water and raced toward me on the current. When it passed within reach I plucked it from the stream, fascinated by its color and promise. In that single leaf I saw all that was to come in the weeks ahead, when the hardwoods burned as bright as candles and golden tamaracks smoldered in the swamps. It meant duck blinds and grouse guns and deer camp and wood smoke, and all the many things I associated with fall.

People ask why I begin searching for fall weeks before autumn arrives. They think it has to do with a lust for hunting, but the real reason is far more ethereal—I'm looking for Brigadoon.

Unlike the fairy tale land that emerges from the Scottish mists for only a day every hundred years, Brigadoon returns for me every autumn. When it arrives I feel intensely alive; it is where I would stay if that were possible. In the same way a restless compass needle is stilled by the pull of magnetic north, the magic that is autumn tugs at me and keeps me steady.

Two weeks later I was back on the Brule. Now every maple shined with patches of yellow and tangerine. Birches were brassy, acorns were falling, and teal were moving in large flocks along the stream. Beavers were busy among the aspens; gnawed trees lay like jackstraws everywhere. Here, too, the earth was spotted with white paint—a sure sign that woodcock were on the move.

At Black Pool the cedars leaned out from the banks to form a canopy over the stream. In the whiskey-clear water every pebble was visible and distinct. I stepped into the river and felt the press of water that was as cool as ice. I moved into position, cautious as a cat, keeping a low profile as I tossed a spinner toward the cedars.

I saw a flash of color through the amber water as the fish struck. The brown came up and when it did my heart skipped—

it was a big fish, and I battled to keep it away from the sweepers. The brown was as red and rusty as cedar duff, and at eighteen inches was the largest fish I'd ever taken at Black Pool. It was a perfect ending to summer.

To be sure, summer was over, but autumn had not yet arrived. When it did the skies would be filled with the tolling of geese, and maples would blaze like lanterns along streams too cold to wade. Ice would rim every pothole in the morning, and ringnecks would come into decoys, unafraid. Coho salmon would be leaping sandstone ledges, and later still steelhead would begin their upstream run. The excitement that was autumn was a long time in coming, but it was worth waiting for and dreaming about for much of the year.

Ten days later I wandered down to the river. The water was low and the fishing had fallen off. I caught and released two tiny browns. Summer was over.

Blue asters and goldenrod were blooming in old meadows, forming solid carpets of blue and gold that would color the land until it snowed. Dry birch leaves lay deep along the trails, and in an aspen copse I found a freshly spent shotshell. I picked it up and held it to my nose, pleased by its familiar odor. Another man might have only caught the scent of gunpowder, but I'd found something more.

At the bridge I stopped for a last look at the river. Along the banks the bracken ferns were brittle and brown. Downstream, a ruffed grouse burst from the dogwood and sailed away through the stark aspens. I hurried across the bridge to Brigadoon.

TWENTY

Firelight

Nothing in the outdoors draws people together as does a campfire. An open flame, deep in the woods, casts a spell that cannot be explained. There are no strangers in a group of people who share the warmth of an open fire, though names and faces may be new and unknown. Around a campfire all men are brothers; like a light in a window, it welcomes us home.

Some fires enkindle contemplation or quiet conversation; others blaze with merriment and outlandish revelry. Yet even when nothing is said or done, there is still much that goes on among friends who share a campfire.

One of these was a fire at the end of Minnesota's Sawbill Trail, a favorite jumping-off point for the vast, roadless canoe country that lies to the north. We reached Sawbill Lake at dusk and pitched our tents in a stand of enormous pines while an icy, late-September drizzle mired us in muck. The trunks of the trees were black with rain; the gray lake had the dreary and lifeless look of slate. Teeth chattered as we quickly built a fire beneath a sodden tarp. Our soggy tents sagged like wet clothes hung on a line.

It should have been a dismal camp, yet the sight of our sputtering campfire held the gloom at bay. Sitting beside the fire, uninsulated from the elements, the talk turned to the extended fishing trip we had planned. Not far away lay Canada, and all around us were thousands of wilderness lakes to roam and explore. Although others had passed this way before, whatever lay ahead would be new to us.

There was no telling what we might find; we only knew it was sure to be more exciting than the familar routines and mindless habits of everyday life. Suddenly we were keenly aware of what the first explorers must have felt in setting out across a young America. We stared into our campfire as they had stared into theirs, filled with the sense of freedom and anticipation that men have always known when venturing toward the undiscovered. Our campfire was a link to those early frontiersmen and a common bond for us. That night, in firelight, we were more than mere companions—we were *adventurers*, setting out toward the unknown.

Other fires I'll always remember are the tiny, trailside fires I shared with my son, Nick, when he was barely big enough to cast a line. He was ten years old and for much of that autumn we fished the run of coho salmon on the Brule. On Saturday mornings we'd leave home with a small pack filled with disposable packets of fruit juice and cheese sandwiches wrapped in aluminum foil. We'd wade the river together below the Lenroot Ledges, catching fish as silvery and iridescent as starlight, before the sun cleared the treetops to burn away the frost. Around noon we'd stop for lunch and I'd light a small, five-minute fire, on top of which we placed the foil-wrapped sandwiches. The bread always charred, the cheese never melted, and the packaged fruit juice was as warm as bath water. These little lunches and their fires weren't necessary, but they were important—they were Nick's first experiences with a way of life that was the only legacy I had to give.

For Nick, each one of these trailside fires was a little adventure. He would search out the perfect spot to stop and rest, gather the small twigs and curls of birch bark, and shield me from the wind as I struck the match. Ordinarily Nick abhorred charred toast, but beside our fires he ate the blackened sandwiches with gusto!

One day he asked to light the fire himself. I gave Nick the matches and stood by as he arranged a handful of dry twigs and rusty pine needles as carefully as if he were building a blind. The fire took on the first match, and when the flames came to life the look of satisfaction on Nick's face was as bright as a beacon.

"I did it, Dad!" he cried. "I did it!"

Suddenly I was a boy again, kneeling in the duff beside the first fire I ever built with my own hands, filled with a joy and sense of accomplishment that I have never quite recaptured. I also knew that in the years ahead, whenever Nick thought about the things we used to do, he would remember our Saturday forays and trailside fires. Somewhere among his memories those fires would always burn brightly, and whenever he thought of them he would think of me.

Those of us who fish the wild places can remember the past by the campfires we've kept, and each of us carries a memory of a campsite and fire that burns brighter than all the rest. Things of quiet importance have happened at such times and places—things that only close friends can share; and while friends and places may vanish with time, our memories of those campfires never fade.

For me, one of these places is Deep Lake, a blue expanse of wilderness water. Along the south shore, sheltered by giant pines and great boulders, is a tiny, quiet bay where David and I watched many campfires. This place belongs to David.

David was an artist who cared more for the sweep and color of a land, and for the way that sunlight plays on water, than he did about catching fish. Yet he was always the first to throw in with me whenever I planned a wilderness trip. His favorite task around camp was tending the fire, and many nights I watched as he sat in firelight, capturing the wilderness with a pencil and sketchpad.

Late one autumn, just before freeze-up, we carried our canoe into Deep Lake. The bluebills were moving, the threat of snow was real, and the bare, empty woods confirmed the feeling that no one was left in that land to disrupt its sense of wildness and isolation.

Our plan was simple: to paddle to the bottlenecked mouth of the bay and fish for the giant pike that would be feeding on the spawning runs of ciscoes. We shoved off and paddled out into a gale, but the wind and waves soon forced us back to the sheltered south bay.

I felt the lake's gray spray at my back as I secured the canoe beyond the reach of combers. David was already building a fire. We sat between the fire and a granite wall, cozy and warm and out of the wind. Snowflakes began to fall as David set a pot of coffee on the fire. Overhead, the wind ripped through the pines while foam-flecked waves crashed against the shore.

There, safe and sheltered from the storm, I felt as close to the natural world as anyone could. We sat back against the granite wall, warmed by the fire, and watched undulating skeins of distant geese battle the wind. The sky was filled with their mournful tolling.

"There goes Christmas dinner," I said. "Too bad we didn't bring a shotgun."

David shrugged. "I'd rather watch 'em than eat 'em." He cupped his hands around his eyes and looked out across the lake, where flocks of bugling geese were rising from sere, brown beds of rice. "It's enough for me to just be here when they're calling. Sometimes I almost think I know what the geese are sayin'." He grinned, sheepishly, as if he'd said too much. "I suppose you think I'm as silly as a goose."

"Yeah, but I'd never tell you that," I said. "You'd probably take it as a compliment."

David smiled. I looked at him as the firelight revealed the joy in his eyes. He had the happy look of a man who was doing exactly what he wanted to do, in the one place where he would rather be than anywhere else in the world.

"If there's a life after this one, I hope it has geese," he said. "I can do without a lot of things, but I sure would miss the sound of those honkers."

Six months later David was gone. That was ten years ago, and I've not been back to Deep Lake. Instead, I like to think others have now discovered that sheltered bay where they, too, listen to the lonesome tolling of geese in November while sharing the warmth of a fire with a friend.

To be sure, campfires are as different as the people who build them, but the friendship enkindled by their light is everlasting. Once a man has been a part of that—once he has known the warmth, the intimacy, and sense of belonging that is always there when friends share a campfire—he can never be alone.

Every campfire is a kind of milepost, like blaze marks along a trail. They illuminate the miles already traveled, and the distances still ahead. Nothing is more companionable than firelight; nothing feels more natural than to share it with a friend. Lakes, rapids, and portages may be forgotten, but the memories illumed by firelight never dim.

TWENTY-ONE

Far Horizons

In the old days, the vast expanse of woods and water that now lies at the heart of Wisconsin's Sawyer County was the ancestral hunting ground of the Santee Sioux. But in the 1700s, the Chippewa—led westward by the Megis Shell of their legends—drove the Sioux from the valley and made it their own. Yankee loggers from Maine and Vermont soon followed, leveling the great stands of white pine and damming the rivers to float out timber. In their wake, settlers and speculators rushed in to claim the land, followed by the fishermen of the late 1940s.

Nowadays, most of us know this area as the Chippewa Flowage—Wisconsin's largest wilderness lake. Created in 1924, when the Northern States Power & Light Company dammed the Chippewa River, the flowage covers 17,000 acres. This sprawling realm of tall timber, dark water, floating bogs, and windswept islands is now managed by the Lac Court Oreilles Chippewa, the United States Forest Service, and the state of Wisconsin. It is also home to world-record muskies.

Most people think of the "Big Chip" in terms of summer, but for a long time I had dreamed of visiting it in autumn—to explore

its immense waterways and far horizons by canoe when few people were abroad. Furthermore, I had decided to make this a solo
journey deep among the flowage's silences. In most places today
it is impossible to know what Marquette experienced in discovering the Mississippi, or to recapture what La Salle felt in ex-
ploring the Great Lakes. But in autumn, on the Chippewa
Flowage, it can still be done. Here, the wilderness still lingers.

My original plan was to put in at the south shore landings,
but always the wind had its way, driving me back to shore. I ques-
tioned my decision to make this trip alone—two people in a canoe could paddle through these autumn winds, but alone I
didn't have that stability or power.

In the end, I headed out to the region east and southeast of
Big Timber Island, near Cranberry Creek Narrows, Cranberry
Lake, and Cedar Swamp. On many maps, it is the only officially
designated canoe route on the flowage, a link between the East
and West Forks of the Chippewa River. Sheltered by islands and
bays, it would provide protection, and being federal land I would
be free to camp anywhere.

So it was that on a Friday afternoon at the end of September
I found myself standing on the shore of Cranberry Lake. I followed a meandering, two-track logging trail known as Forest Service Road #1604. At the end of the trail the world of towns and
roads felt far away.

I pitched my tent in a clearing beside the lake, collected firewood, and then went down to the lakeshore, hoping to catch
supper—or a muskie. The setting sun tottered like a red ball
above the crown of a distant island. The wind had lost its bluster
and in the twilight the only sound was the swift whisper of wings
as flocks of wood ducks passed overhead. I tossed a leech-tipped
jig into the tea-stained waters, hoping for a walleye. The rock
bass I caught instead were delicious.

*   *   *

In the morning, before the sun had burned away the mists, I
loaded the canoe and paddled north, hugging the shore. West of
Cranberry Creek I made good time, traveling in the lee between
the mainland and a long island. There, in the calm, I tossed a
bucktail spinner, expecting nothing, but secretly wishing for one
of the Big Chip's fabled muskies.

Muskellunge—or muskies, as they're commonly called—are the
pinnacle predator of North America's freshwater food chain, as well
as the premier game fish of the Northwoods. Wisconsin produces
most of them, and the largest come from the Big Chip. Built like a
barracuda and tough as an ax handle, muskies are famous for their
aerial antics and ferociousness when hooked. Up to five feet long
and seventy pounds in weight, you occasionally hear reports of
100-pound fish turning up in the backcountry. I have seen muskies
attack and devour young geese and muskrats, and more than one
tourist has lost his toes by tangling his feet in the water from the end
of a pier where a muskie was lurking. It wasn't too many years ago
that fishermen kept pistols in their tackle boxes to shoot the monsters before bringing a hooked muskie into the boat. Yet for all that,
they are the most difficult fish to find and catch. It's said that it requires 10,000 casts to catch one muskie. Nevertheless, there are le-
gions of anglers who fish for muskies exclusively.

Muskies and the Big Chip are inseparable, and the mystique
of the fish exerts its influence on the flowage and on all who visit
there. It was here where Cal Johnson and Louis Spray launched
their famous quest for a world-record muskie, the two battling
both the elements and each other as they searched for a giant fish.
In 1949, Spray won the contest by landing a gargantuan muskie,
an almost mythical fish of sixty-nine pounds, eleven ounces. Even
now, more than fifty years later, it remains the world record.

I fished for muskies in the flat water west of Cranberry Creek for two hours, running out of patience long before I made anything close to 10,000 casts. Connecting with a muskie requires a single-mindedness of purpose I don't possess. To me, the *act* of fishing matters more than the catch.

The serious pursuit of fish and the act of fishing are only peripherally related, like spirituality and sanctity, or love and sex. One is a challenge calling for real effort; the other is an effort to avoid challenges of any kind. One angler casts his line at fish; the other fishes to kill time. The serious angler may catch muskies; if I'm lucky, I might catch a nap.

*   *   *

The sun was climbing into a blue sky filled with white clouds, and shorelines were luminous with the first blush of autumn colors. Rafts of diving ducks rode waves like roller coasters, and overhead a lone bald eagle soared high against the blue. On shore, a doe stood mesmerized as I glided across her reflection before flicking her white tail and bounding away.

Ahead lay a half-mile of open water, and beyond that, Big Timber Island. Foam-flecked combers marched across the open water: once I was into those rolling whitecaps there would be no turning back.

I adjusted my load to ride as low as possible in my canoe, planning to paddle north and ferry westward toward the island. It was risky, but the blustering beauty of the Chip made me bold. I left the sheltering calm and pointed my bow into the wind.

A hundred yards from shore the wind drove me to my knees, which was an efficacious posture for the prayers I started to recite. I'd bitten off more than I could chew. The bow rose on every wave and fell with a sickening slap as it hit the rolling crest beneath it. I paddled furiously, trying to quarter into the wind to keep the canoe from swamping.

Big Timber Island loomed straight ahead, a world away. My arms were aching, yet my progress seemed to be one of inches. And then suddenly I was much closer to the island, and I could hear the hiss and spray behind me as I entered the leeward waters off a tiny tongue of land. The worst was over—I had made it. Then came the thrill that wilderness travelers relish after having challenged—and beaten—the elements. So much for avoiding exertion.

I beached the canoe on the island and ate a lunch of cheese and crackers while boiling water for a pail of Darjeeling. As I fed the little fire, a blue heron floated down from the sky to land in the shallows where enormous, hollow stumps stood like castle turrets. These stump gardens are everywhere on the Chip—a clue to the size of the trees that once cloaked this land.

I sipped my tea and studied a map of the flowage, bemused by the odd place names: Spooky Bay and Hell's Half Acre; Moonshine Lake and Pork Barrel Island; Camp One Creek and Pine Point. Like the stump gardens, they told of an era of peaveys and axes—a time so near in the past it felt as close as my shadow.

After lunch, I headed south, sheltered from the wind, toward a fleet of islands that loomed like schooners in the distance. It was a leisurely trip with the time and freedom to fish, and at the end of Big Timber Island I saw a muskie.

It was in the shallows, on the shady side of a stump, looking as long and dark as a shark. I had an enormous, red-and-white Creek Chub Pikie Minnow tied to my line—a lure about as large as your average brook trout—and I pitched it far to the side of the fish, letting it sit until the ripples stopped. Then I began its retrieve, cranking the reel's handle in short, erratic spurts—maybe a bit too erratically.

The muskie burst like a rocket from cover, coming up from under and behind the lure, breaking free of the surface, and seemingly tossing my lure up into space. The fish had missed the bait. In a moment it was over—the muskie was gone—and the Pikie Minnow floated lifelessly on the surface. But for a long time the turbulence caused by the muskie rocked my canoe. I swear that fish was 10-feet long and 200 pounds. Well, maybe 180.

*   *   *

On a whim, I boarded a floating bog, though a misplaced step might have meant disaster. There are scores of such bogs on the Chip—floating mats of sphagnum and heather, studded with black spruce stubs and tamaracks. These islands drift like rafts manned by phantoms, moving wherever the wind deems. I ran the canoe's bow up on the heather and stepped gingerly on the floating mat, the muskeg soft, spongy and quaking with every step.

Wild cranberries hung like tiny red lanterns at the edge of the heather. Cedar wax-wings and mallards were feeding on the fruit, as well as one lone red squirrel that somehow had been set adrift on the muskeg mat. I picked a few berries and winced at their tart, citrus-like taste, and then collected enough to cook that evening in water and sugar over a campfire. I would eat some of the mixture immediately and pour the rest like syrup over pancakes in the morning.

Late that afternoon I pitched camp south of Cedar Swamp, where the flowage is little more than a river above the Winter Dam. I sat in the twilight as beavers fed in a patch of pond lilies, the animals ripping up the cable-like roots and then clasping the stalks in their paws, like kids eating stick candy. Otters were play-

ing and mallards hurtled through the dusk, while back in the timber owls boomed and brush wolves bayed. It was a mélange of
sounds as old as the North itself—the timeless call of wilderness.

I sat on a log in the last light and thought about my solo trip.
In autumn, the Big Chip is almost too big for one man in a canoe,
but I wouldn't hesitate to do it again. Its far-reaching waterways,
distant headlands and lonely islands teem with excitement when
summer ends. If you go, you may not experience it exactly as I
did, but somewhere among its solitudes, you, too, will know the
thrill of far horizons.

TWENTY-TWO

Lost Lake

Long before I ever saw it, I dreamed of discovering Lost Lake. Of course, "Lost" was only the name I gave it, and anyone else who ventured there was free to call it what he liked. Lost Lake appeared on only a few maps, and then only as an unnamed spot of blue surrounded by roadless woods. But this was the sort of anonymity and isolation I was seeking.

In those days, when I had only myself to think about, I would go off into the woods at every opportunity with the hope of discovering my mind's image of the perfect wilderness lake. I wanted to find a lake where time had no meaning, and where silence and solitude were vast. I also wanted a lake where the fishing would be virginal. This should have been easy to find in a place like Wisconsin with its 15,000 lakes, and many times I thought I had found it, but always in the final analysis something was missing, some nebulous and nameless quality I could not define but which I quickly recognized when it was lacking.

One day, in early September, I wandered far beyond the reach of roads and became lost among enormous hemlocks that stood like cathedral colonnades. Then the big trees fell away, a broad horizon opened up, and ahead lay the blue expanse of Lost Lake.

Boulders as big as pickup trucks littered the shore, lying in the same spot where the retreating glaciers had dropped them, eons ago. A pink, granite ledge gleaming with rose-quartz jutted out over water as clear as crystal. From that ledge I could clearly seek northern pike as big as fence posts, finning along the lake's gravel bottom.

I was trembling as I cast the Dardevle. One of the pike turned and smashed the spoon like a wolf striking down a doe.

I gave a shout when I pulled back on the rod and felt the solid set of the hook. Soon I was on my knees, scrambling to pin the pike to shore. It was, at the time, the biggest fish I'd ever caught.

All that autumn I visited Lost Lake. I was always alone, and for all I knew, I might have been the only person to ever visit Lost Lake. And though that was unlikely, it felt that way just the same.

I built a birch bark lean-to where I could camp on the ledge and fish for pike, feeling as free as Huckleberry Finn. I was too young to understand that I had discovered something more than good fishing and a wilderness lake. I only knew that at Lost Lake life was worth living.

Eventually those weekend outings became day trips, and even these stopped. Years passed between visits. Yet whenever I went back, the lake remained exactly as I remembered it.

When my son Nick was ten, we hiked in to Lost Lake together, for the first time. And on his first cast, he hooked a two-foot northern. I stood beside him, cheering.

Even after we released the fish, both of us were shaking.

"No matter how many pike you catch, each one is like the first," I told him. It was the same way I felt about my visits to Lost Lake.

*   *   *

It doesn't seem possible that that was a decade ago. But my graying hair, expanding waistline, and the wattle where my jaw used to be confirm it. Time is a babbler, said Euripides, and speaks even when no question is asked. I don't look in mirrors as much as I used to.

This past summer, when I turned fifty, I tried to calculate how many days in my life were spent fishing. My "guesstimate" was 5,000. Yet, when I try to recall all that time spent on water, the only days that are absolutely clear and in focus are the hours I spent at Lost Lake. I don't know why this is, except that even now the promise of visiting Lost Lake fills me with excitement and anticipation. Maybe it's because it's the only place I know of where nothing ever changes.

Last week, just before Nick left home for college, the two of us wandered back to Lost Lake for the first time in years. The hike in was more exhausting than I recalled; I had to stop to catch my breath. The experience was more than just new and unsettling.

To be sure, Lost Lake had weathered the years better than I had. The shores were still wild, the icy depths still crystalline and blue, and the great hemlocks stood as timeless as ever. I peered into the mirror images of its surface, expecting to see the reflection of a man past his prime. Instead, I spotted a gigantic northern pike.

In an instant I was a boy again, quivering as I hurled the red-and-white spoon. Nick saw the fish as I tried to make it strike, but after my second cast the big northern turned away. Later, on the long walk home, Nick said that just seeing that enormous pike was reason enough to come back to Lost Lake someday. I agreed. It's the fish you haven't caught that keeps time at bay, and makes life an adventure worth living.

TWENTY-THREE

The Wind in the Wire

In autumn, when I'm out in the woods with a rod or gun, I often get sidetracked by the lure of abandoned places.

It happens whenever I stumble across an old mining camp, a deserted sawmill town, a vacant farm or an empty cabin. For a little while I'll forget about the trout or grouse, and sift through the ruins searching for relics.

But I should know better.

Wherever I find an ancient cant hook or rusty lantern, there, too, I always find the tragic tale of artifacts.

Any angler or hunter who has ever visited an abandoned farm, and listened to the wind whine in the wire of an old stock fence, has known that feeling of melancholy and sorrow. It's the price you pay for poking around in places where people's dreams came to an end. Spend enough time listening to the wind in the wire and eventually you become a different person: you stop seeing yourself as being something more substantial than stone, and realize that all men are only shadows.

It was that way for me the day I discovered Orienta. In the old days it had been a lumberman's town, standing on the red-clay bluffs above Lake Superior, at the mouth of the Iron River.

In those days, an ancient pine forest rolled away, unbroken, from three sides of the town, the trees so large and their canopy so thick that in winter the sun in the southern sky never rose above the forest crown.

It was the pines that brought the sawmill to Orienta, and it was the dreams of the settlers that made Orienta a town. Scandinavian immigrants who came by schooner were encouraged to take jobs in the mill and surrounding logging camps, or to hack farms out of the slash of the cutover land. There was talk of building a grand theater, where stars such as Helena Modjeska, John Philip Sousa, and Lillian Russell might be persuaded to perform, and rumor had it that the Northern Pacific was prepared to lay track all the way to Orienta's back door.

Then one morning the people of Orienta discovered there were no more trees to be cut into logs for the mill. The vast forest that was to last for a thousand years had been leveled in a single generation, and now the ravaged slash rolled away, unbroken, to the far hills. Schooners arrived, and the loggers loaded the ships with the last stacks of lumber, while millhands disassembled the twin saws of the mill. Then the schooners turned toward the northeast, bound for Chequamegon Bay, leaving behind a sawmill that had no saw, and a town that had no future.

Seventy years later I was hunting ruffed grouse along the main street of Orienta. The wilderness had returned, and now the land was as alone as it used to be. The old road was flanked by the mature spruce of the second-growth forest; it lay in the trees like a bad wound that had healed itself long ago.

On both sides of the road square depressions marked the graves of old homesites, the crumbling foundations overgrown in aspens and hawthorn brush. It looked like a fine place for grouse, and when I stepped off the trail a pair of birds burst from a blackberry thicket, streaking through the trees for the river bottom below.

I followed the birds down the sunny slope to the stream, hoping for a shot. Then I saw it: the big stone walls of the mill, hidden in the alders and black ash of a swamp. The weathered walls of the mill had the look of an ancient fortress, and the sight of it tugged at me like lantern light luring a moth. Now all thoughts of hunting disappeared: there was only the old mill, and the secret past it concealed.

Inside, the dust and duff of forest debris lay seventy years deep on the floor. The smell of the past was rank and musty, and when I touched the doorway the stone wall had the icy-damp feel of a tomb.

In one corner stood a table built of square timbers, littered with leaves, and with tin cups and plates once used for the millhands' meals. Nearby, hanging by hooks from a wall, were the men's tools, the wrenches and blacksmith hammers still in their places. I picked up a rusty bolt, and when I did I could hear the whine of the saws cutting lumber, and the calls of the millhands shouting over the din. I could smell the odor of sweat and oil, the fragant piles of fresh-cut sawdust, and I could feel the suffocating heat of working in that place among the machinery on a stifling summer day. I looked down at the bolt that was staining my hand with rust, and then suddenly and without any warning, I could feel myself being caught up in an immense sadness.

Perhaps it was the old mill's sense of immediacy: the dishes ready for the millhands' noon meal; the hammers and wrenches still in their places; the stone steps clearly etched with the marks of hobnailed boots. It was as though the men of the mill had stepped outside for only a moment, and now, almost a century later, the mill was still waiting for their return. At such times perceptions are easily altered: life becomes less like a river and more like an endless lay of land, where the lives of men pass like the shadows of clouds, and where your own lonely shadow is lost among them.

I felt that way one autumn in the canoe country north of Ely, Minnesota, when I discovered the ruins of an old settlement near the Echo Trail. I'd been catching smallmouths on a remote lake when I decided it was time to get out of the canoe and stretch. I walked away into the brush toward what looked like an old homesite. Nothing remained but a few fieldstone chimneys, the chimneys rising from the autumn woods like the weathered obelisks of a lost civilization.

There was something cryptic and ghostly about finding the chimneys in a place where only the deer ever wandered. They were one of those mysteries that haunt the North—a riddle whose answer I would never know. Some were massive as monuments, while one chimney looked as though dwarfs had built it for a gingerbread house. The only clue to their history was an inscription chiseled into the base of one fireplace. It read: "This be our hearth and family's heart."

In reading the words I also read something of the man who wrote them. Whoever he had been, he had once taken time from the hardship of making a life in the wilderness to put into stone some record of his dreams. Both the man and his cabin had vanished long ago, but for me he was no longer a phantom. He was someone who had loved his family deeply, so deeply that his love was still there, scrawled in stone, expressing itself to the weather and wind.

I saw, too, that although you may love a land, and sink your roots deep into its soil, your presence is nothing more than mist on the water unless there are others with whom to share your dreams. For the wind blows, unnoticed, through the ruins of Orienta, while the wilderness has reclaimed the chimneys of the Echo Trail, and the sadness is not in seeing that those places lie forgotten, but in knowing that no one remembers the men who once lived there, and the hopes and desires they sought to make real.

Another time, my friend Rick and I spent a few days in the Brule River country. Early in the mornings we made sets in the marshlands, where wood ducks and mallards streaked in low over the bogs; later in the day we'd fish for steelhead and salmon.

One evening we made camp along a stream below an abandoned farm. As was the case on other deserted homesteads in that wild backcountry, the former owner had purchased the land from logging companies after the big timber was taken out at the turn of the century and tried to raise corn on soil that yielded only pine stumps and rocks. No one had lived there in over fifty years; still, painful reminders stood like monuments to futility.

Tiny meadows, handwrought from the slash, now lay overgrown in brush. Old fencerows marked where the farmer had laid boulders after spring clearing, and where the second-growth forest now gained another foot of ground with every passing year. At the front porch of the house a lilac bush had spread and gone wild. And behind the house, concealed in young aspens, was the simple gray marker of a child's grave.

We camped among some fieldstone cairns beside the bank, where someone had once tried to fashion the rocks into crude stone chairs. The wind was backing around to the northeast, and we moved our blankets close to the campfire. In the twilight we listened to flocks of bluebills come whistling down the stream.

"Hear that?" Rick would whisper each time the ducks moved above us in the dark. "Come morning, we're gonna have some shooting!"

But I couldn't think about the hunting. In the whistling sound of bluebills I seemed to catch an echo of that place, and of the way it had once been when the woods were filled with the sounds of life and laughter. It was easy to imagine the farmer coming down to the stream at the end of a day, sitting on the cool stone chairs in the gathering dusk, and trying to trick the river's native speckled trout into striking. It was easy, too, to imagine the hopes he and his wife held, and the simple joy she must have felt in seeing her lilac bush bloom each spring, full of promise for the future. And yet I could also imagine their agony in clearing rocks each year to grow a crop too meager for their needs, and the heartbreak of finally yielding to the punishing nature of the land, and the pain of having to give it up with a child buried in it. I realized then that no one man can ever leave a lasting mark upon the land, but that a land may leave its mark upon an individual forever.

In the morning we paddled over to the marsh where the first big flights of bluebills passed within range of our guns. Long before the sun cleared the trees our game bag was filled with scaup; we loaded the decoys and turned toward camp.

After our gear was packed and loaded, Rick and I took a last walk along an old fenceline to the farm's abandoned house. Now it stood empty and vacant and battered, but I tried to see it as it once was, when smoke climbed from the chimney and the lilacs were in bloom. But it wasn't any good. All I saw was a human drama lost to oblivion, a tale that had ended years before I was born. I looked at the sturdy old house, built to last forever, and again I felt the farmer's sorrow. It made me want to reach back through the years and touch his shoulder in a simple, uncomplicated act of compassion, in the way you might comfort a friend when his world turns ugly and bleak.

"You look at this place, and it's easy to feel sorry for the people who lived here," Rick said. He shook his head. "I feel like I knew them, but I don't even know their names."

We listened to the wind wailing in the rusty wire of the fence-line. In it was the sound of that place, and a thousand broken dreams.

Those who look at a hunter and see only violence cannot imagine he may be a man easily wounded by the past. Yet a hunter, more than most, knows the world is a place of shadows, and that life is more tenuous than dew in a spider's web. Those who call him a brute and savage would do well to visit the abandoned places, where the wind is always tolling like a bell for human hopes. For nothing is more dangerous in our shadowland world than the man who fails to see he is only a ghost.

TWENTY-FOUR

Listening and Watching

I used to belong to a sportsmen's club whose members were known by nicknames—names that indicated each man's area of outdoor expertise. I tagged along with guys who had monikers like "Gander," "Buck," and "Steelie" in the hope of discovering my own area of expertise and, in the process, earn myself a nickname like the others. I succeeded, too—although I wasn't all that fond of being called "Slouch."

In truth, I'm not lazy so much as I'm only ordinary. But in a world where everyone is striving to be an "expert" at something, the things an average outdoorsman can brag about are small change, indeed. Admittedly, it'd be nice to take the time and learn all the snooty Latin names for trout, or how to lay a spread of decoys that look real enough to lay eggs. But in the world of outdoor life I am "the voice of one crying in the wilderness"—usually because I'm lost and hoping someone will hear.

I'm the guy in the next blind whose duck call sounds like a Bronx cheer. I'm the walleye fisherman whose shore lunch is a toothpick. It's not that I'm too lazy to learn the tricks and techniques that others use to take fish and game. My problem is priorities: instead of learning *how*, I'd rather wonder *why*. As a result, most of my time afield is spent in listening and watching to the small, the trifling, the fleet.

Years ago I used to fish with an expert angler nicknamed "Hawg." I admired Hawg's skills in catching bass, but even when we shared the same boat, the gulf between us was as wide as Hudson Bay. While I poked around at the bottom of a bait box, trying to decide which nightcrawler looked the luckiest, Hawg would discourse on spoon-plugging, back-trolling, structure fishing, jigging and popping. Until then, I'd always thought fishing was as simple as breathing air.

Hawg never understood why I would pause at dusk—just as the largemouths began to bite—to watch mallards sail across a mandarin sunset, or to marvel at how a lake's untroubled surface could reflect more than trees and sky. He was mystified as to why I was just as pleased in catching dimunitive crappies as he was in battling hefty bass, and he had absolutely no patience with my lame attempts at mimicking loon calls. When Hawg went fishing, he went *fishing*. To Hawg, it was something serious, highly technical, and—from the look of it—the arbiter of his joy and despair. But for me every day on the water was a little adventure, where I was free to watch and listen to whatever was there. Hawg may have caught fish, but I found wonder.

Nowadays, during duck season, I've taken to leaving the blind an hour before dusk, just as the mallards swoop into the rice beds for the evening. By then I've taken a token bird or two, and while I understand my companions' desire to keep shooting until limits are reached or the last, legal minute of hunting hours has expired, I also understand that other mallards and duck blinds—years from now—are at stake.

Usually I'll walk away and follow some logging trail into the jack-pines and scrub oaks. On a good day, I may kick up a partridge and finally take a shot without being ridiculed for missing. But far more often I just walk away from everyday cares and watch the twilight's vanishing shadows race through the woods toward the sunset.

To the extent that it's possible, I try not to think; like a goofy Zen bum from a Jack Kerouac novel, I seek only to be aware. And so I simply watch and listen—for the swooping shadow of an owl, the distant yapping of coyotes, or a faint rustling among the brittle pines and scrub oak—was that a porcupine, or a bear? Occasionally, I think about the earth beneath my feet, still rebounding at the rate of one inch every hundred years from the crushing weight of glaciers that receded from this land 10,000 years ago. Or I may stare, awestruck, at the mile-high tolling of geese, aware that their journey's end is as mysterious to me as my own destiny. Idle thoughts for idle forays. Yet, there in the purpling dusk, I encounter meaning.

Like the narrator in the opening lines of Dante's *Inferno*, I find myself at the midpoint of this mortal life, gone far astray from the path that once seemed so direct. By anyone's standards my accomplishments to date are unexceptionably ordinary, and all the evidence suggests my future will be a repeat of the past. That's why I've come to believe that if I'm to leave a lasting mark on this world, I'm apt to do it out-of-doors without much fanfare.

I have a friend who exemplifies this. For twenty years he fished the fall run of steelhead on the Bois Brule River, never once catching a fish, largely because his casting technique resembles a blind man swatting at flies. Last November he was caught up in admiring the way sunlight plays on the big pool below May's Ledges when something rolled in the water near the end of his line. His rod was nearly ripped from his fist.

"You've got one!" I shouted.

It was obvious he had tied into an enormous steelhead. The fish dashed downstream like a runaway freight. I nearly swallowed my pipe when it jumped clear of the water. The size limit on steelhead in the Bois Brule is twenty-six inches. This fish was as long as my arm.

The net was barely big enough to hold it. I couldn't tell which of us was more stunned. My friend goggled at his catch, his wide eyes magnifying his joy. After twenty years and untold hours of idly casting to the Brule, he had caught the fish of a lifetime.

After I removed the hook from the steelhead's jaw, my friend admired his fish for a moment more. Then he released it.

"You could have kept it," I said.

My friend shrugged. "I don't have any money to leave my kids," he said. "But maybe I can leave 'em a few trout."

If I've learned anything for all the aimless hours I've spent in listening and watching, it is this: ordinary people who idle away time in the out-of-doors learn things that ambition never knows. They discover that fishing and hunting have nothing to do with getting and taking; that the things they cherish can be easily lost; that sportsmanship is another word for self-sacrifice; and that real success lies in what they freely leave behind for others to find on another, far distant day.

"Everything great is not always good," said Demosthenes, "but all good things are great."

Because of my predilection for listening and watching, the spare room that serves as my den holds far more pine cones and curious stones than it does mounted fish and game. But each of these items represents a time or place, when, for a brief instant, I caught a glimpse of my true niche in the cosmic scheme of things. It has to do with preserving the thrill of wonder for future sportsmen I will never know, and a belief that by sparing a few ducks and fish for distant tomorrows, even an ordinary person may accomplish great things.

TWENTY-FIVE

The Lonesome

He was an old man in baggy waders and a mackinaw that had seen better days. I wondered what he was doing there, alone in the dark, kneeling on the shore of a wilderness lake. It was late November, the temperature was below freezing, and a full moon filled the snowy woods with its glow. He was working by the light of a driftwood fire, scooping up fish he had netted with a seine.

"My name is Thomas," he said.

He was the last thing I expected to find at that hour. I'd spent the day jump-shooting mallards near the Namekagon. Afterward, I took my time walking back through the dark along an old logging trail, savoring the icy silence of the frozen forest, and the sense of isolation that comes to the North just before the first big snow. Near the trail's end I passed a lake that was almost split in two by a peninsula. At the end of that point the old man's fire filled the trees with a glowing nimbus.

"I come here every November for the ciscoes," he told me. "Just before freezeup is the only time to catch 'em."

I watched as Thomas scooped up ciscoes from his net, placing the fish in a couple of five-gallon buckets. They were small, silver fish, no bigger than perch. But what they lacked in size was offset by quantity—the sleek, little fish filled one of the pails to its rim.

"I roll the little ones in batter and fry them like smelt," said Thomas. "The bigger ones I cook like brook trout."

"It's been a long time since I've seen anyone seine for ciscoes," I said.

"You weren't supposed to see me. I thought I was alone."

Evidently, Thomas was a "cisco kid"—a member of that most clandestine class of fishermen. They seine for ciscoes on the darkest and coldest nights of autumn, when no one is abroad to disrupt their lonely pursuit. But this arcane atmosphere only adds to the cisco's mystique.

Without a doubt, the cisco is the mystery fish of the North. A first cousin to lake trout, ciscoes spend much of the year at the bottom of deep lakes—lakes sixty-feet deep and more. Summer anglers never see them. Ice fishermen sometimes catch them, but seldom in numbers to make a meal. However, in November just before lakes freeze, their nocturnal spawning runs bring ciscoes inshore to shallow water. Anyone with a seine or dip-net can take dozens of ciscoes at such times. The abundance of ciscoes is reflected in the fishing regulations of northern states. In Wisconsin, the daily limit is twenty-five pounds!

"It's better when two men drag the net," said Thomas. He looked down at my feet. "You're wearin' waders. Wanna give it a try?"

I looked at the old man's furrowed face. His eyes searched the lake for something I couldn't see.

"Look!" he cried. "Ciscoes!

Ciscoes threshed and rolled across the surface of the shallows, their tails and backs out of the water, creating a long stream of turbulence in an otherwise placid lake. Thomas hurried to the water's edge to free the seine from where one end of it was anchored in the brush. I set aside my shotgun and mallards.

We each took an end of the seine and waded out into the black water. The lake's bottom was firm, and I could feel the seine's weight scrape across the sand. Thomas stayed inshore while I headed for deeper water, testing each step with my toes. I didn't want to slip into a muskrat run—even in my neoprene waders, the press of icy water made my legs ache.

The seine began to jerk as ciscoes hit it.

"We're into them," Thomas called.

Faraway, a timber wolf howled.

Seining for ciscoes is unlike anything else. The mechanics of it are a lot like seining for smelt, but the pleasure is more sublime. In spring, when smelt make their runs in the upper Great Lakes, there's a sense of unbridled hoopla: crowds set up camps on popular beaches, and campfires blaze through the nights with merriment. Smelt fishing is fine sport and a communal affair, an excuse to socialize after the long isolation of winter.

But cisco seining is a solitary pursuit. There's a quiet excitement in being alone with a wilderness lake on a snowy autumn evening, with miles of frozen silence pressing in from every side. The dark silhouettes of spruce trees stand like mute sentinels on sable shores, illuminated only by a campfire, a cold moon, and the distant light of stars. It's a lovely, lonely world that belongs to owls and wolves, and to men who never feel so comfortable as when they're alone in the woods.

We scooped the fish from the seine and into a bucket, built up the driftwood fire, and peeled down our waders. We rolled cigarettes, struck a match, and lay back against a cedar log. Thomas passed me a fresh pint of ginger brandy. I broke the seal, held up the bottle in a toast, and took a swig of brandy so corrosive I thought my esophagus would dissolve. I passed the bottle to Thomas while I searched my pockets for Pepcid.

"Tell me about yourself, Thomas," I said.

The old man shrugged. "Not much to tell. I got a place on the Namekagon and keep to myself."

He stopped to see if I was listening. I was.

"Used to be plenty of us that seined for ciscoes," he said. "In those days a man *had* to—if he was going to feed his family. I'd net so many ciscoes, the kids and me would stack 'em frozen, like cordwood, in a shed. My kids are grown now, scattered everywhere but here."

An owl called from the dark timber across the lake. Thomas looked away in that direction.

"Folks have it better today," he said. "Nobody needs to net ciscoes anymore. Now I mostly come here for the memories . . . and for the lonesome."

Thomas cocked his head, as though he were listening for something.

"Hear that?" he asked.

I strained to hear what Thomas was hearing, but all I sensed was profound isolation and the miles of icy silence. We were utterly alone.

Thomas grinned. "You hear it, all right," he said.

We filled the final bucket with fish and carried our gear out to the road. We split the catch and made a date to meet again the next evening. But although I kept our date, Thomas never returned.

He didn't return because I think Thomas has already found something more companionable than people. It has to do with the darkest and coldest nights of autumn, when owls call and timber wolves howl, and when men who never feel at home in a crowd drag nets through northern lakes, listening for the lonesome.

TWENTY-SIX

The Talisman

It was only November but the sky above Lake Superior had the look of winter. Snow was falling on the Canadian side of the lake, and the radio promised that my corner of Wisconsin would be buried by morning.

This time the snow would stay. There had been other storms, brief forays by winter into November's gray woods, but afterward the sun came out, temperatures climbed, and the snow melted, leaving the woods wet and brown. But this time the snow would stay, cloaking the earth in a thick, white mantle.

Winter was hours away, yet I wanted one more chance to visit autumn. Snow would soon obliterate it. Its lakes and streams would freeze, and then the year's fishing would be only a memory. Before then, I wanted to take something of autumn into winter's inanimate isolation—a spirited image I could keep and recall when icy winds beat against my windows and snows lay deep against my cabin's walls.

I headed upstream along Muskeg Creek, through a colorless forest of black spruce and white birch. Dry leaves littered the trail like scraps of parchment, each leaf speckled and downy with frost. During the night the creek had frozen over; now the stream was as rigid as stone.

I was looking for autumn, but autumn had vanished. Gone were the rustlings of animals and birds, the calling of geese, and the cooing of swans. The abandoned woods teemed with quiet expectation—a sort of anxious, restless hush, as if everything were waiting for the snow.

Suddenly I felt a drop of something wet and cold against my face, followed by another and yet another. Ahead, in the gray light above the creek, the air was white and hazy with snowflakes. Down they came, settling into the curl of fallen leaves, the furrowed bark of logs, and on the frozen stream. Snow was gathering in patches on the forest floor. The silence, too, had changed. Now there was the almost imperceptible rustling of falling snow.

*   *   *

As I grow older I become more aware of the first snow. Its arrival not only signals a change in seasons, but also the end of another year, and the advent of a time when life hangs in abeyance, as inert and stark as a skull. Ahead lies long months of killing temperatures, when the frigid air is too painful to breathe and trees explode from unbearable cold. Time is no longer a matter of schedules, but of survival.

Activity is stemmed as darkness enfolds the earth for most of the day. Some creatures pass these long nights in slumber, but others are addled by the dark, lured away from safe dens by the false light of a winter moon. Yet in the morning, in the snow, there are always signs—the carcass of a rabbit ripped asunder, the blood-flecked trail of a lynx—that those who are deceived by darkness risk dissolution.

Northern winters can be hard on fishermen. If you're retired, you might join the winter convoy of gray-haired anglers who begin their journey in Duluth at the top of I-35, traveling all the way south into Texas, Mexico, and even Belize in search of open water. The rest of us have to stay here and look at their photographs when they return.

Some of us who stay while away winter by taking up ice fishing, sturgeon spearing, fly-tying, or rod making: others visit the traveling sport shows that make the rounds of northern towns in midwinter, collecting travel brochures for summer fishing camps that keeps us in reading material until May. But none of this is an adequate substitute for casting a line into open water. To an angler, it's a lot like dancing with your sister.

My friend Finnish Bill spent winters in solitude at his 10 × 12 trapper's shack. Snowed-in for months all alone and miles beyond the nearest road, he passed the time by hauling slash onto frozen lakes. He'd stack the brush in piles, binding it all with baling wire to which he attached gunny sacks weighted with rocks. Working on snowshoes and skis, it often took him weeks to build just one of these brush piles. Later, when the lakes thawed in spring, the piles sank to the bottom, creating the backwoods version of a fish crib. Even now, years after he's gone, I still catch bass and crappies near his submerged brush piles.

Another man I know steals into his neighbors' woods and shoots squirrels. He takes only the tails, leaving the carcasses for the ravens, and sells the tails to fishing tackle manufacturers for twenty-five cents a piece. This same poacher cuts aspen saplings, about an inch in diameter and twelve feet long, for "dummy fishing." In summer, he adds a few feet of fifty-pound-test braided dacron line and a wire leader, attaches an enormous treble hook on which he impales a twelve-inch sucker, and rigs an empty, gallon-size bleach jug to the line to serve as a bobber. He hangs this off the back of a jon boat, using an electric trolling motor to cruise muskie lakes until he gets a strike. Once the hook is set, he tosses the whole thing—pole, line, and gallon jug—into the water. Every time the muskie dives it encounters the resistance of the floating jug and aspen pole. The fish exhausts itself trying to break free of the resistance and eventually floats to the top, belly up, where it's easily scooped with a net. All the poacher has to do is follow the bobbing jug until it stops. He sells the fish to visiting "sports" who haven't caught a muskie and don't want to return home empty-handed. Lust is more easily satisfied than love, even in fishing.

Incredibly, the poacher and Finnish Bill were brothers. They grew up together on their family's backwoods farm, working side by side even as young men, until the poacher married and Bill relinquished his share of the farm as a wedding gift. I can't explain how two men with so much in common turned out so vastly dissimilar. One of them was sunny, giving, and trusting; the other grasping, grim, and dark.

"He changed when he lost the farm," Bill once told me in talking about his brother. "The bank took everything, and then his wife left. It broke his spirit."

Maybe. I do know that Bill approached fishing with the humility of a repentant sinner entering a church. When his brother went fishing it was to steal the poor box.

*   *   *

I came out of the woods where a dirt road crossed Muskeg Creek. Snow had already covered the gravel, leaving the road immaculate and white. Wet, heavy snowflakes fell in a boundless swarm. Small drifts were already winnowing on the frozen stream.

Then I heard it: a soft, muted gurgling, barely audible above the rustling snow. From the bridge I looked upstream. Below the rusty railing, water was bubbling up through a hole in the ice. It lay below a ledge, where the current was just strong enough to keep the water open.

I peered into the lambent creek. Illuminated by the snow and ice above it, the streambed literally glowed. I could see white pebbles lying on the bottom, and green strands of something like watercress weaving in the current. The quick water stirred up little swirls of gravel. Dead leaves and twigs floated away.

A shadow slowly materialized beside the watercress. It wasn't until the fins moved that I realized it was a fish. It was a tiny brook trout, barely longer than my finger, the scarlet spots along its flanks gleaming like rubies. It was finning wildly to keep its nose pointed upstream and remain rooted in the current. Occasionally it would turn as the fast water swept it away downstream beneath the ice, but within moments it was back, fins waving madly, determined not to yield.

Snow was falling all around me and the weight of winter would soon crush every living thing, yet here was irrepressible life.

I'd found what I'd gone looking for. In the days ahead, whenever I felt the press of winter's pall, I would remember the defiant brookie shining brightly at the bottom of its snowy pool, a quick and lively sprite amid the encircling gloom. The image of the little fish bucking the current would be my talisman against winter's darkest days. Ice, killing cold, and unrelenting snow are formidable elements—but no match for the vivacity of brook trout and the fishermen who love them.

PART FOUR

WINTER

TWENTY-SEVEN

The Wishing Well

Ice fishing has to do with simple things and simple pleasures, but most of all it has to do with hope. That is the reason why some men brave the bleakest days of winter to spend hours on a frozen lake, peering down into a hole.

In Wisconsin fair-weather anglers dream of muskies, but in winter the biggest fish a man can hope to catch is a giant northern pike. Because the biggest pike are taken on tip-ups in winter, I look forward to ice fishing with all the expectation of a child listening for the sound of sleigh bells on Christmas Eve.

I look forward to the long, lazy hours spent with friends in a warm place indoors, making plans about where the group of us will fish next weekend. I like the way no one bothers to bring up the weather at such times, though we know—more likely than not—it will be unbearably bitter and cold. I like the primitive gear and the idea of carrying everything you need in a bucket, or hauling it behind you on a sled. I like the wide, white expanse of a frozen lake, and the way sun dogs blaze above the horizon. Most of all, I like the simple thrill of peering down into a dark-green hole and knowing that somewhere beneath the snow and ice lurks the biggest pike I will ever know.

Once the holes are cut and the tip-ups are set, there is no other activity in all the outdoors where time can be spent more leisurely. It is the only one I know of where a man can sit for hours, doing nothing, and still feel that something vital was accomplished. It is also one of the few situations in which a group of people will come together and no one will feel awkward if the conversation abruptly ends. Out on the ice, staring down into a hole, a man is free to be alone with his thoughts, even in the company of friends.

Except in rare instances the fishing is never frantic, and the long lull between strikes provides a handy excuse to build a fire. It's a chance to open the waterproof match safe I always carry but otherwise never use, and to feel like a real woodsman capable of living well in any situation. Building a fire in the snow with frozen wood is a test of outdoor skills, and even the act of gathering the wood is somehow satisfying and fills a need to live with the land. And later, after the tinder takes and the kindling ignites, there is always the sense of having won another small victory.

Those fires are what I remember best about ice fishing as a youngster: small boys have no patience with staring into empty holes. A bunch of us would start an old stump on fire along the shore, tossing in anything that would burn, and toasting skewered pieces of blood sausage or hot dogs, simply to have something to do.

Sometimes one of us would catch a perch and that would get roasted, too. When it was cooked as black and brittle as our wet leather mittens, five or six of us would divvy it up into tiny slices, carving it as carefully as a Thanksgiving turkey. Along with the perch, our wool socks and rubber boots usually went up in smoke, because one of us was always trying to prove something by inching out on the black ice around a pool of open water.

One time the group of us fell through the rotting ice near a spring hole, and before we could make it back to shore our clothes froze and turned stiff and rigid as cardboard. But that was all right with us—falling through the ice and nearly drowning only justified our building an even bigger fire. That was long ago and nowadays my own son comes in from ice fishing with charred socks and burned mittens, but I think he knows my reprimands are empty, because a part of me will always be out there on the ice, wet, cold, suffering from frostbite, and basking in the warmth of a fire and friendship.

I like the sound of a winter lake "making ice," and the way everyone pauses to listen. I like the terrible, bestial moaning as the ice expands and cracks, and the quiet terror I feel whenever water erupts from an open hole as a crack splits the ice beneath my feet. After all these years, the uncertainty is still there.

I like the shanty towns that pop up on some lakes as soon as the ice is safe to travel. I like the cozy feeling of sitting in a warm, dark shack, and the way your eyes reel at the sudden burst of sunlight whenever someone opens the door. I like the excitement that follows when the bright flag of a tip-up unexpectedly springs skyward, and the mad dash across the ice to reach it, as friends shout, "*Fish on!*"

An ice fishing shack is a fine place to visit with friends. After the first hour of initial tension and anticipation, everyone begins to relax as it slowly becomes evident that the fish have disappeared. Even men who ordinarily have little patience with small talk engage in it at such times. A tar paper shack, out on the ice, is no place to express profound thoughts or provocative beliefs. Instead, it's a place for simple and idle banter; a place to joke about the weather or the comic misadventures of other days; a place to trade ideas that are no more complicated than an ice spud; a refuge in a pretentious world for unassuming men.

My old friend, John, was one of those men. Old John was a weathered woodsman who lived alone in his trapper's shack near the Iron River, and for many winters the two of us often fished Lake Superior's Bark Bay. John had no patience with the ostentatious. His ice fishing outfit consisted of two snuff boxes: one filled with hooks and sinkers, the other packed with bait. He carried a spool of black, braided line in a pocket and kept an ice ax cached in a snowbank near the lake.

Bark Bay and its slough was wilderness water then, and we always had it to ourselves. John would pick a spot, seemingly at random, and then begin hacking holes through a foot of ice. For a break he'd wander off and come back with a few, spindling sticks of ironwood, and rig them with line into makeshift jigging poles. Small fish were thrown back or cut for bait. Big fish were threaded through the gills and mouth and carried home on a forked stick. Although we occasionally caught a wandering splake or steelhead, John's real quarry was northern pike. The fish he took were often enormous: pike as big around as sawbolts and as long as a man's leg.

At seventy, John was more than three times my age, and he relentlessly referred to me as a "young pup." But he delighted in sharing his secrets of backwoods ice fishing, and I always pumped him to learn more. When the waxworms ran out, he'd tie a crude fly from the red wool of his mackinaw and use it to make panfish bite. For shore lunches, he heated two flat rocks in a blazing fire, and then swept the coals aside to cook the fish between the rocks. Sometimes he brought along a coil of bell wire to set snares for snowshoe rabbits, or, when the pike were hitting, he used it to make leaders and then fashioned crude tip-ups from popple wands and patches from an old, red bandanna. But mostly John taught me that even during the short, bleak days of winter, there is no end to the things a man can do outdoors. All that's required is hope and imagination.

Of course, a lot of what we did was simply *waiting*—waiting for the holes to be chopped, waiting for the fish to bite, waiting for the fire to start, waiting for one of us to finally admit that he was cold and wanted to go home. Yet we always went back at the first chance we had. Even the waiting was something to be savored and enjoyed.

We waited by getting down on our knees, cupping our hands around our eyes, and peering down into the holes. At first there was nothing to see, but slowly we grew accustomed to the dark water so that we could look farther and deeper into the lake until the bottom suddenly materialized like an image in a dream. And a dream it was.

Beneath the ice lay a gleaming world of magic. Somehow sunlight pierced the prism of snow and ice so that the lake bottom came to life and glowed more luminous than the moon. It was a sunny world of alabaster rocks, ivory shells, and silver logs, and of strange furrows etched in pure, white sand. An invisible current weaved its way unseen beneath the ice, rustling the silent eel grass and milfoil like trees in a wind. It was a lot like looking down on a landscape from a mountaintop, a magical land where dreams could come true. Because of this, every baited line I dropped into those depths was like a coin tossed down into a wishing well.

Perhaps it was because I always had the feeling that something was going on down there beneath the ice, something secret and mysterious and just outside our field of view. I always believed that if we watched and waited long enough, it would pass beneath the window of the hole and we would finally learn what the ice concealed. In my mind it was a northern pike, the biggest and most fearsome in the world.

But if that fish was there he never showed himself, and because of that, ice fishing now means more to me as I grow older.

Because none of the fish I saw back then—or have seen since then—is why I go ice fishing every winter. It is that one, great fish I hope to find—that giant pike that lurks somewhere beneath the ice in my imagination—that lures me away from home on winter days when sun dogs blaze above the horizon.

Ice fishing has to do with simple joys and simple pleasures, like sharing a fire and being with friends. But more than this it has to do with the always sunny world of expectation, a world of wonder and wishes, where hope never ends.

TWENTY-EIGHT

Red Camp

The cabin known as Red Camp stands along Lost Creek in a roadless area of the Lake Superior country. Named for a logging camp that stood on the site eighty years earlier when the last of the big pines were leveled and taken out, it was built by a trapper out of what he could salvage from the old logging camp's abandoned buildings. He ran his lines from the shack, stringing sets along streams like the Reefer, the Iron, and the Muskeg. But by the time I discovered Red Camp, it was again abandoned, used only by outdoorsmen seeking shelter for the night.

Not long ago, when winter snows lay deep, I made a call at the cabin. I wanted to see the rugged log walls chinked with moss and clay, and look out from the shack's solitary window at the tall spruces rising like fortress walls along Lost Creek. Most of all, I wanted to experience once again the elemental world of Red Camp.

I packed my rucksack with the few things I'd need for the night; I also tossed in a box of teardrop jigs and a matchbox filled with sawdust and waxworms. Then I loaded the .410 in case I jumped supper along the trail and turned my snowshoes toward Red Camp.

The beaver ponds along Lost Creek were thick with ice and shrouded in snow. I shuffled along a portage trail once used by Indians, the same trail where ten years earlier I had met a young trapper who ran his sets over the corduroy country of ridges and rivers, spending his nights at Red Camp.

All that winter, whenever one of us visited the shack, we would leave behind some small gift for the other to find: a candy bar, a box of tea, a full match safe, and always a supply of kindling and firewood. These small things meant much after traveling long miles by skis or snowshoes through a winter wilderness. But more than this, there was pleasure in knowing that—at least at Red Camp—the simple courtesies of an old and better man-nered world were still intact.

Once, unintentionally, I left behind my copy of *Walden* at Red Camp. The book was still there when I returned months later. Inside the cover, scrawled on a scrap of paper, the trapper had left this note: "It sounds like Thoreau spent time at Red Camp."

Built of logs stood on end and spiked into place, the shack had the appearance of a pioneer's stockade. Daylight shone through cracks between the logs where the chinking had fallen away. The roof was a latticework of dry spruce poles, over which someone had once placed half-logs and birch bark. As cabins go, Red Camp was as natural as a wigwam.

When I revisited Red Camp recently I was delighted to find that nothing had changed. The bunk built of rough-sawn planks remained spiked to the rear wall. The barrel stove was still in its place, its rusty tin chimney riddled with miniscule holes through which tiny plumes of smoke escaped. Nearby was a galvanized bucket for fetching water or snow. On a single shelf, stored in a metal canister, were all the essentials: matches, a candle, and the last ten pages of a catalogue.

By no stretch of the imagination could Red Camp be called beautiful: it was as crude and austere as a dry spot under a tree. Yet it was this primitive quality that lured me back. Here, far from modern life's confusions, my thoughts were uncluttered, my perceptions were stark, and I felt as close to the wild as a wolf. I came here for the same reason Thoreau had sought out Walden Pond: to drive life into a corner and recapture its simplicity.

I started a fire, fetched a bucket of snow, and set that and my canteen near the stove. Then I grabbed one of the many spuds left behind by innumerable pulp-skinners over the years, and punched a few holes through the creek's ice. I tied a teardrop jig to a handline, baited the jig with a couple of waxworms, and then jiggled the lure just off the stream's bottom. I caught and released two perch, both little bigger than my thumb. An hour later, with the sun beginning to set and no fish for supper, I walked back to the shack for the shotgun.

I took the .410 into the spruces behind the cabin. In minutes a snowshoe hare burst from a drift. My first shot bagged a clump of red osier. My second bagged supper.

Later, after the cooking things were cleaned and put away, I stepped outside. The night was brilliant with the ancient, icy light of stars, the constellations so bright they looked near enough to touch. The woods were silent but for the murmuring spruces and the groans of the creek making ice. In the distance timber wolves were howling. Here, far removed from the familiar and routine, life was an adventure.

I went back into the shack, lit a candle, filled the stove with dry aspen, and crawled into my sleeping bag. I lay awake, watching candlelight flicker against the log walls while deer mice rustled beneath my bunk. I looked up and saw the moon gleaming through a gap in the birch bark roof. Red Camp was more than a change of pace. It was a change of worlds.

TWENTY-NINE

Pine Knots

A forester will tell you that a pine knot is only a chunk of solidi-fied resin. He will tell you a pine tree has resin ducts through which its sap flows, much in the same way veins and arteries in a human body carry blood. But in some places the flow of resin is stopped, as if dammed by a tourniquet. Usually it happens where branches spring from the main trunk. Later, after the tree falls to the ground, the trunk and branches will decompose. But where the sap has pooled at the pine knots, the wood remains inde-structible. Impregnated by resin and solid as stone, these chunks of pine wood will remain intact for hundreds of years.

Because of the concentrated pitch, the wood burns as bright and hot as the arc from a welder. I have seen pine knots burn out the bottom of a barrel stove, and many times I have tossed a pine knot into a campfire at night, only to find it still burning as a solid chunk in the morning, hot enough to boil coffee and fry bacon.

People will tell you a pine knot is useless. It cannot be cooked to make a meal, cut like tin to make a patch, peeled like pulp to produce a dollar, or mounted like a deer's rack to adorn a wall. Yet every pine knot is a thing of wonder, and, in a very real sense, a capsulized history of the North.

Many of the pine knots lying undiscovered throughout the North came from trees that were already old when Cartier sailed for the new land in 1534. These scattered remnants of the past have witnessed a long march of succession as Indians and explorers, miners and loggers, settlers and sportsmen played out their roles in the history of the last five hundred years.

Most of the pine knots in my woodshed were collected while trout fishing backcountry streams. I have one pine knot that came from a stand of ancient trees that once stood guard along the Bois Brule River. The trees were part of the vast pinery that mysteriously took root in the upper Great Lakes after widespread fires destroyed the existing vegetation in the 1400s. These trees were later leveled during the logging boom that lasted from about 1880 to the 1920s.

I found the knot under the duff of a "cradle-knoll"—those elongated mounds of earth that resemble graves grown over in second-growth timber. Before the loggers, the pines of a virgin forest were left to lay wherever they fell after succumbing to old age, disease, lightning, or wind. Left undisturbed, these toppled monarchs began to decay and were eventually buried by forest debris. At the end of a hundred years a fallen tree might be only dust, and the only evidence to show it ever existed was the elongated mound of the cradle-knoll, marking the spot where the trunk had crashed to the earth.

My pine knot comes from a tree that may have provided shade and a resting place when Daniel Greysolon, Sieur Du Lhut, ventured up the Brule in 1680, searching for the Northwest Passage. I like to think the famous explorer paused to smoke his pipe beneath the tree that rendered my knot, and each time I look at that knot I catch a glimpse of the same wonder he must have felt in seeing the great trees, and in traveling through a land that was still young and filled with mystery.

Further east, along the Presque Isle River, there still stands a tract of massive white pines which date back to a time before the Chippewa. The pine knots concealed there are among the oldest that still exist, and the history they offer reads like a mist— unfathomable, unknowable, a secret world. One of the knots I've collected from the place may have once been part of a branch from which cougars ambushed their prey, and which served as browse and shelter to caribou and elk. Phantoms from another time and place haunt the shadows of that forest; yet, through the pine knots I've found there, I've been able to hold time in my hand and reach back through the mists to touch that primitive world.

The smell of a burning pine knot is as fine and fragant as the rarest incense, and the light and the dreams that a burning knot will produce has a quality and beauty unequalled by any other wood. The outdoor writer Gordon MacQuarrie knew this when he wrote: "You cannot shoot a pine knot, or eat it, but it is a lovely thing and makes a fine fire. . . . Until you have your wood- shed awash with pine knots, you have not ever been really rich."

Tonight I'm sitting before the open door of a stove into which I've tossed a pine knot. Sparks leap like crackling stars from the bubbling resin, while the flames burn with the color and dizzying brilliance of the Northern Lights. The knot was once part of a tree that rose like a phoenix from the ashes of great fires that swept over the North in the time of Columbus, and tonight, five hundred years later, the last bit of that tree is burning in the fire of my stove. Soon it will be only ashes, and in a few days I'll spread the cinders over the snow and ice on the dirt drive that leads to my cabin; and in spring, the start of some new, green thing will begin to grow where the cinders fall.

Ashes to ashes, dust to dust—such is the lot of both pine knots and fishermen. And in the flame of my pine knot tonight, I see the light that burns like a lamp in all living things; a fire that shines brightly for only a little while before turning into smoldering ash, only to wait for its chance at being fire once again— a fire that may change its heat and form and intensity, but which never fails, and which can never be extinguished.

THIRTY

Northern Lights

Crazy Gus lived alone in a 1952 Chevy school bus that he had purchased in Oregon after returning from Vietnam. He was twenty-three at the time. A week later he wandered into a Spokane tackle shop, spent the rest of his separation pay on a bunch of outdoor gear and beer, and then started fishing his way across America. He'd been reading Richard Brautigan. The bus threw a rod after crossing the St. Croix, rolling to a stop in the woods near Loon Lake. Thirty years later Gus was still living out of the bus which now included a woodstove and a lean-to. The lean-to was built of discarded plywood and car hoods.

Last night Gus dropped by, unexpectedly. He'd made the two-mile trek from Loon Lake on snowshoes, in temperatures cold enough to cause frostbite.

"The walleyes were biting tonight," he told me. Gus opened his pack and showed me five golden fish, each about fifteen inches long. The walleyes were solidly frozen from his walk.

"Took 'em all minnows," Gus said. He reached into his coat—a ragged, red-and-black wool mackinaw that he had picked up for $2.00 at the Goodwill store in Duluth. He pulled out a jelly jar half-filled with pickled shiners.

"Why don't you use 'em and try your luck tonight?" he said. "You know where the gear is cached. Use the bus and spend the night. I'd go with you, but I gotta bring these fish to the Widow."

The "Widow" was the forty-something daughter of the logger on whose land Gus's bus was permanently parked. She and Gus had been an on-again, off-again item for years.

I poured a few rounds of Jameson for Gus to "warm up." Even without the whiskey he would have been talkative. Afterward we went outside and I watched as he bound the snowshoes to his feet.

"I can give you a ride to the Widow's," I said.

"Nah, it's too nice a night, but thanks." He looked up into the icy light of a million stars. The full moon was bright enough to cast shadows.

"Just look at all that beauty," he said. "Do you ever wonder where it comes from?"

I didn't say anything, so Gus simply shrugged, bashfully.

"Guess I'm talkin' through the side of my head again," he said.

I watched as Gus shuffled off into the night, heading cross-country for the Widow's house, a mile away. Long after he was gone from view, I could hear him singing among the silent balsams. Gus might have been a bit crazy, but he was one of the happiest people I knew.

*   *   *

It was a beautiful winter night, soundless and clear. The temperature was hovering just above zero. I wasn't up to making the trip to Loon Lake and fishing in the dark, but the night was too lovely to spend indoors. Besides, Gus had started me thinking about things, and I wanted to put some distance between me and my thoughts.

On a whim, I took the skis and broke a trail down the length of the lake below my cabin, making my run under the bright and icy stars. It had snowed a little just before sunset—a light powder that flocked the balsams and greased my skis. Now, in the moonlight, the snowy balsams glistened.

It was too cold to travel slowly and I pushed hard against the sticks. The only sounds were my laboring breath and the hiss of my skis. At the far end of the lake I stopped and turned around. Ahead, in the moonlight, was the black silhouette of my cabin. Wood smoke rose from its tin chimney in a straight, unwavering plume. There was no wind, no sound of things in motion, no calling of animals or owls, only the silence of a late winter's night.

Slowly, above the northern horizon, a smoky, pale shadow began to pulsate—a pool of murky, green light that had not been there before. In the next instant, a quaking column of color fell from the sky, bursting like a bomb above the horizon and exploding into the breathless beauty of the Northern Lights.

The aurora raced from east to west above the frozen, snowy lake, the sky a shimmering curtain of misty yellows and greens. Trembling, ice-blue streamers rippled like banners from one end of the sky to the other; ethereal waves of red and orange fell in cascades. Gone was the familiar light of moon and stars: in their place was a weird, uncanny luminosity that gave the whole night a sense of unreality. At times the lights swelled with brilliance before fading to a muted glow, but then they were back, brighter than before, swirling and spinning in forms and patterns that sent my imagination reeling.

The spectral lights were otherworldly. Shafts of frosty light shot up into the air like wild, scanning searchlights; the spiraling cartwheels of the merry dancers streaked across the sky like comets gone amok. The lake itself boomed and cracked, as though the ice were being torn asunder. As far as I could see the lake was snow covered and icebound, and yet, at the limit of vision, below where the aurora burned brightest, I had the impression that a rift had opened in the earth, from which beams of eerie light emanated from its fiery interior. The night was filled with magic and mayhem. It was a world other than my own.

The Northern Lights have always hinted at the supernatural. The old Chippewa believed the lights were the ghosts of the dancing dead, while the Vikings saw them as the Valkyries—the handmaidens of Odin—ferrying fallen warriors to Valhalla. Even now there are a few old Finns in the Lake Superior country who think of the aurora as Turja's Rapids—the blazing gate to Tuonela, the underworld of Finnish mythology. The Finnish composer Jean Sibelius captured something of this in his haunting piece *The Swan of Tuonela*.

But for me, the Lights epitomize that lonely and mysterious land of black spruce, white birch, and gray winter known as "The North." The Northern Lights are as much a part of that country as the land itself. They are also a part of every man who has ever watched the aurora and wondered.

Now, standing on skis and leaning against my sticks while gazing across the frozen lake at the northern horizon, it was easy to believe that the supernatural was at work. Spiraling lights climbed like wraiths through the air, spinning wildly and weirdly, changing shape and color, and always climbing higher until they were directly above me. There they burned like mauve and purple flames, so near they seemed to hiss and crackle. The snow-covered earth all but reflected the rosy resplendence; the very trees and hills were aglow.

At such times life reveals itself for what it is. I have known such moments in the autumn darkness just before dawn, when wild rice beds stood sere and soundless, and the swift whisper of bluebills passed unseen in the dark above me, as I waited in a blind, alone with my thoughts. Another time I discovered it at dusk while standing on a ledge above a tremendous canyon, listening as silence filled the void until the purple chasm was all but brimming with the hush. And once I found it near the bustling Loop of downtown Chicago, when I ducked into an empty church to escape the clamor. There, amid the quiet beauty of flickering candles and streams of stained-glass light, I made contact with the same silent splendor that lies at the heart of wild places everywhere. At such moments I am always most aware that I am linked to something that defies comprehension. Now, gazing at the Northern Lights, I felt that sense of profound mystery once more.

I vaguely remember what we learned in school about the cause of the aurora—something to do with solar flares, exploding gas molecules, and electromagnetic radiation. But it was only a theory, as spellbinding as a discourse on P/E ratios. Astrophysicists could keep their colorless explanations; I preferred enchantment.

"Just look at all that beauty," Crazy Gus had said. *"Do you ever wonder where it comes from?"*

Suddenly, I felt guilty for ignoring Gus's question—or worse, for having been too proud to reply.

Now, watching the final sortie of the Northern Lights, I marveled again at the wonder of the aurora. Shafts of light were rising in a final, violent climax, draining color from the sky as faint flames of green flickered in the North. In an instant, the magic was gone. I thought about the warm bed waiting for me at the cabin, and turned my skis toward home. The winter lake was again soundless and white, illuminated by the moon's familiar glow. And I was back from the spirit world of the Chippewa, the Valkyries, and Tuonela, and from the simple and infinite beauty that is the Northern Lights.

THIRTY-ONE

Polaris Descending

I'd been fishing through the ice near the mouth of a river, just beyond where winter welded the stream to Lake Superior. The fishing had been good and I kept three splake trout for supper; the fish lay scattered like cordwood in the snow. Now it was time to head home. The western sky was pink and apple-green. Along the shore, silver birches shined like rapiers in the last rays of light.

It was dark before the last of my gear was packed, and with the darkness the temperature plunged into a deeper cold. The frozen fish in my canvas sack felt as heavy as bricks as I climbed the bluff above the lake. I stopped for a break at the top of the palisades, watching the evening's afterglow burn away like embers.

Overhead, the big sky was alive with the bright light of the constellations. To the south lay Orion, the Great Hunter, stalking Taurus, the Bull. To the North was the Big Dipper, part of the Great Bear. Every orb and planet was ablaze, creating a vast, celestial wilderness of wonder.

It's surprising how lost most of us are when gazing at stars. While almost everyone can locate the Big Dipper, even most outdoorsmen do not know where to look for Polaris, the North Star. And in all my life I've met only a handful of people who could point out more than three or four of the constellations.

Perhaps it's because we're born with a sort of interior short-sightedness. We look at a lake and see only water; we walk through a forest and see only trees. When we pause to look at things—if we ever pause at all—we see only what is apparent, and then often imperfectly.

Five thousand years ago the wandering tribes of ancient Mesopotamia charted the course of their caravans by the light of Thuban. In the seemingly static skies of their own time, Thuban was the North Star. But today Thuban is only another star, largely forgotten; instead, Polaris has replaced it as the North Star, and those of us alive today believe Polaris will always be there to guide us. Yet, in another few thousand years, a star in Cepheus will replace Polaris.

Now you see it, now you don't. Such is the state of stars and existence, and trying to glean meaning from what we see is impossible if we discern only the obvious. "How little do they see what is, who frame hasty judgments upon that which seems," wrote the poet Robert Southey. To appreciate what is really there—whether it be the stars in the sky or the trout in the next pool—requires something more than sight.

*   *   *

Tremendous changes have come to fishing in recent years. This is evident in lower creel limits, mandated catch-and-release, slot sizes, closed seasons, banishment of natural baits, and a glut of other measures designed to protect the resource while affording maximum opportunities for recreation.

Many believe these changes result from the end of a natural abundance that until now has been our legacy as Americans. Even if this were true, the end of abundance is merely an effect and not the cause of its own destruction. Until the fishing public sees itself for what it is, regulations will grow ever more restrictive. An effect is similar to its cause.

Nevertheless, my enthusiasm for fishing remains undiminished. If we can land men on the moon, we can surely correct or contain the many threats to sport fishing. All that's required is mighty endeavor. For all that has been tarnished and lost, I continue to believe, like Thoreau, that "the wildness and adventure that are in fishing still recommend it to me." Only those who come to fishing with no other aim but to catch and keep fish would think otherwise.

To be sure, catch-and-release isn't always painless, but it is often right. And just as surely, the chance to keep a reasonable number of fish is essential to fishing; without it, fishing is nothing more than hunting with an empty gun. But "reasonableness" itself is endangered. In an age when political correctness is mistaken for virtue, our superficial culture has so eroded ethics that many anglers confuse "sportsmanship" with owning the latest fashion in graphite rods and GORE-TEX clothing.

Catching fish is not the measure of fishing. It is clean, uncluttered lakes and free-flowing rivers, silence and solitude, history and tradition, good company and good manners, and the promise—however remote—of discovering a secret stretch of stream or a backcountry lake where a man can be alone and remember what spirit means. Unfortunately, this is *not* the view of the many.

There is such a thing as a zeitgeist or "spirit" of the times, and ours is materialism. People believe only what they can see, and seek satisfaction in things they can measure. In fishing, this manifests itself in bigger boats and motors with more noise and damaging wakes; more technology and less real contact with nature; more roads into remote places with ATVs, SUVs, and crowds everywhere; and more fish caught and killed for the sake of a photograph.

Polaris is slowly descending, unnoticed, into oblivion, and lakes where one man used to catch ten trout in a year are now visited every weekend by unknown numbers of people who keep every fish they take—and wonder why the fishing isn't what it used to be.

Now you see it, now you don't.

It all comes down to perception. Those who appreciate all the elements of fishing and the environs in which it takes place will always go home with a full creel—even when they fail to catch a fish. Understanding that determines whether you're a sportsman or just a "sport." It will also determine the future of fishing.

*   *   *

We see very little of what there is to see. I learned this years ago, on a boyhood camping trip. I was stargazing from the open flaps of a tent when my attention was suddenly fixed on the pulsating light of a passing satellite. Hoping to get a better look at it, I grabbed my binoculars. I was not prepared for what I saw.

The sky as seen through the binoculars was not the same sky I had been watching only moments before. While lying in my tent I had seen the trio of dots that make up the Three Sisters, the dot-to-dot images of the Big and Little Dippers, and the shining, bright cluster of Pleiades. But now, looking through the glasses, they were lost. Instead I beheld a universe of light—countless numbers of twinkling, white stars that had not been there before, each one separate and distinct, pulsating with a life all its own. The sheer multitude of their numbers left me breathless. There was no way to focus on any single star and isolate it with a name; instead, there was only light—vast and immeasurable.

When I took away the binoculars the familiar night sky I had always known reappeared. But now it was somehow new and more exciting. Although the immense universe of countless, brilliant stars had always been there above me, I had never been made to feel its presence until the low magnification of the binoculars revealed it.

Stargazing, whether it be done with a telescope, a pair of binoculars, or the unaided eye, is an exercise in expanding our perception. There is no better way for the man who believes only in what he can see to be made aware that his perspective is woefully shortsighted—as is, perhaps, the satisfaction he seeks from the immeasurable abundance that is fishing.

THIRTY-TWO

Paths of Enlightenment

When I was a small boy, my father often speculated about my future. "Yes sir, son, you're destined for great things," he liked to say. "Someday you'll grow up and make all of us proud. Maybe you'll be a doctor or a famous scientist. Heck, maybe you'll even be president someday."

As we soon discovered, Dad was not blessed with the gift of prophecy.

All thoughts of ever amounting to anything vanished from my mind the summer I turned six years old. That was the summer I caught my first fish, and from that moment on I knew what my destiny was.

"I'm gonna spend the rest of my life fishing every day!" I happily announced to the family.

Dad was suitably impressed. "Over my dead body," he said. "No son of mine is going to grow up to be another Ole Svenson."

"Who's Ole Svenson?" I asked.

"He's what happens to little boys who go fishing every day," Mom replied.

"Listen, son: fishing is fun, but it doesn't pay the rent. A bucketful of bullheads won't buy you a bobber," Dad said.

At the time, I appreciated my father's advice about as much as I did a Christmas gift of underwear. Then, a few days later, I visited Casey's Candy Shop.

"How many jawbreakers can I get for this carp?" I asked.

"You get that stinkin' fish outta my store or I'll break your jaw for nothin'," Mrs. Casey said.

It was soon evident I was being victimized by a society in which everyone was expected to work. Yet, from what I perceived, people who held steady jobs seldom went fishing every day. The dichotomy of the situation kept me stumped for several years. Then, when I was ten, I met Ole Svenson.

Ole Svenson was one of those unwashed old-timers who haunted the lakes and woods of Wisconsin when I was growing up. He lived alone in his shack and spent his time fishing, hunting, and hiding from the warden. People said he was useless, never having worked a day in his life, and teachers often mentioned him when illustrating the long-term horrors of illiteracy. My own mother referred to Ole as "the scourge of Christian folks," but to me, Ole Svenson was the perfect role model.

For many years Ole was the smartest person I expected to meet. He knew all about fishing and hunting as well as the names for every animal and plant. Because of this, I spent much of my young life following the old woodsman around while Ole served as my guide and mentor. Whenever I had a question I'd take it to Ole, confident he could solve any riddle.

"What kind of frog is this one, Ole?" I'd asked.

"A peeper!" he'd answer without having to think. "Those peepers of his are watchin' every move I make."

"What makes him jump?"

"Springs," he'd reply. "They got little springs in the haunches to make 'em jump. Why else do you suppose folks call 'em *spring* peepers?"

One day I mentioned to Ole that it was only a matter of time before the world would break me, and that eventually I'd need to forget about fishing in order to find a steady job.

"'The world breaks everyone but afterward many go fishin' at the broken places,'" Ole said.

"What does that mean?"

"I dunno. It's just somethin' some philosopher made up." Suddenly his face broke into a smile, and I could tell by the light in his eyes that Ole had solved my problem. "Say, if you're gonna need a job, maybe you could find work as a philosopher."

"What's that?"

"Them's folks that sits around all day thinkin' of stuff to say," he explained. "From what I seen, a fair share of 'em are fishermen, too. Nearly every fella that ever soaked a worm has got somethin' to say about somethin'. Guess sittin' and thinkin' and fishin' just naturally go together."

"What kind of stuff do philosophers think about?" I asked.

"Oh, stuff like 'A fish in the creel is worth two in the brook.'"

"Who said that?"

Ole looked over his shoulder. "Shucks, guess I did," he said. "Ain't nobody else here but you and me." He took a chaw of tobacco and wiped his mouth on his sleeve. "Okay, boy, now it's your turn to think of somethin'."

I closed my eyes and tried to think the long thoughts of a philosopher. Suddenly my tongue began to move with a life all its own and the words came out in a gush. "If the waders fit, wear them," I said.

Ole slapped his knee and laughed. "By golly, boy, I do believe you got a natural knack for this here philosophy business."

Soon I began reading everything I could on philosophy, from Plato and Pascal to Palooka. Sometimes I had no idea what I was reading, but that was all right, as I was pretty sure philosophers themselves had no idea what they had said. By the time I was thirteen I was into Zen and seeking my first encounter with satori.

I found it one afternoon while helping my father load a new fiberglass canoe. Just as we were lifting it to the roof of the car, I suddenly dropped my end and exclaimed, "If a bass jumps in a lake and there's no one there to hear it, does it make a splash?"

Dad was immediately caught up in the Zen mood of the moment and posed a koan of his own: "If a dumb kid asks stupid questions and wrecks my new canoe, does he run for his life?"

I hit the Path to Enlightenment at a full gallop with Dad in hot pursuit.

Another time I came home and found my father wrestling with the Dialectic Theory of fishing reels. His favorite reel was lying in pieces on a bench, and one look told me he would soon need to purchase another.

"I took it apart to fix it, but I'll be darned if I know how to put it back together," he said.

I was immediately reminded of A. B. Alcott's comment on the subject. "'To be ignorant of one's ignorance is the malady of the ignorant,'" I told him.

After that it was several weeks before I could sit down to read another book.

Yet, more than my reading, it was Ole who shaped the mud of my mind. It was positively amazing what he knew about philosophy for a man who thought Marcus Aurelius was the Latin term for northern pike. Once, while we were fishing a river for smallmouths, Ole suddenly burst into a discourse on the Dilemma of Moral Man.

"Two things fill my mind with wonder," he said. "The number of fish in this here stream, and the number the law says I can keep."

"That sounds like Immanuel Kant."

Instantly Ole dropped down in a crouch. "Where? Where'd you hear him?" Ole whispered as his eyes anxiously scanned the woods. "That guy Kant ain't the new warden, is he?"

At other times Ole would encourage me to join him in his search for meaning. Once I found him looking for it in a copy of the fishing regulations.

"Look at this durn thing," he said, tossing me the booklet. "I bet even the fella that wrote it don't know what it means."

During my senior year in high school Ole and I drifted apart for a spell. That was about the time I met Mary Lou and discovered that there was an awful lot to life that philosophers never wrote about. Curiously, philosophy played a big part in our relationship. Mary Lou claimed she loved me for my mind and its easy grasp of Jean-Paul Sartre. I loved Mary Lou because she was easy, and for the way she could make me feel like an Existential Man. But she broke things off between us the following spring when I stood her up to go fishing with Ole. Despite her passion for Nothingness and Being, she failed to see that there is nothing like being on a trout stream come opening day.

" 'Tis better to have loved and lost, than never to have loved at all," I pined.

"Aw, don't take it so hard," Ole consoled me. "You just take a chaw of this here tobacco and you'll be feelin' better quick. There's more than one carp in the creek."

"Euripides?" I asked.

"Naw, you don't rip it. Just stick it between your teeth and bite off a chaw."

Today, years later, I can't say that being a philosopher has been a bad life, and I now know there was never any other choice. Fishing—and especially the lull between strikes—turns most men into philosophers, and I often wonder to what heights

Socrates might have risen if only he had been able to kill time fishing from a muskie boat. Of course, I'd rather Ole had shown me how to be an oil tycoon or shipping magnate. But with fishing, career opportunities are pretty much limited to philosophy. To be sure, there's always the chance of becoming a big-time, high-stakes, tournament-winning angler, but in my case, I do better at thinking about what I'll catch than actually filling my creel.

When that happens and disappointment taps my shoulder, I think of Ole and a bit of advice he gave me long ago.

"The world ain't nothin' but just one big fishin' hole," he said, "and if you ain't got a line in the water, it don't take no voodoo to see you're gonna get skunked."

Maybe a philosopher could say it better, but I guess Ole knew something about life after all.

Alone in the Woods

The primitive cabin stood at the end of a forest trail. In good weather a 4 × 4 could be driven to within a hundred yards of the cabin's door, but now, in late winter, the rotting snow lay deep, and the only way in was to hike in on snowshoes.

The cabin was to be sold in spring, but before then it needed work: fresh paint, interior repairs, a level porch, new shingles. I had agreed to do the work and to live at the cabin until May; in return, I'd have the chance to experience something few people ever know in our modern world. For six weeks—forty days and nights, to be exact—I'd have the chance to live in solitude beyond the reach of TVs and telephones, newspapers and neighbors. The nearest town lay twenty miles away, separated from the cabin by an unbridged river, unplowed roads, and untraveled wilderness. Until the cabin's owner arrived in May to bring me out, I would be utterly alone.

But I was ready for the adventure. Like many people, I had long harbored a desire to spend time alone in the woods—time not measured by hours or days, but by calendar months. Like Thoreau, I had wanted to find out if I had missed anything by never having lived in solitude. Then, too, there was the promise

of fishing every day for six weeks: steelhead would soon be start-
ing their spring run. But most of all, I wanted the time and space
to pursue uncluttered thoughts. In some vague and sentimental
way, I expected to find answers to life among the solitude of
wilderness.

My personal items filled the three Duluth packs that I hauled
in on a toboggan: warm clothes, a sleeping bag, favorite foods
and books, pencils and paper, tobacco and tea. The cabin was
stocked with enough dried food to feed one man for months,
along with all the fishing gear I might use. There was also a .410
shotgun with a full box of shells and a coil of bell wire for snar-
ing snowshoe rabbits. Tools and building supplies had been
brought in before the first snow. Cans of paint were cached under hay in a root cellar, and the shed was filled with firewood and
kerosene for the oil lamps. The cabin's furnishings, though
rugged, were comfortable, and the bunk that served as my bed
felt as though it had been built especially for me. Everything had
been provided, and I was as happy as a king in his castle.

My first days at the cabin were spent evicting mice and
sweeping out the place while cheerfully ruminating about the
joys of solitude. I ate when I was hungry and slept when I was
sleepy, and I soon realized that if I worked only a few hours each
day, the cabin's repairs would be completed by May.

I was as free as any person could be. I spent long, leisurely
hours reading and writing, or traveling the woods with the .410,
potting rabbits. Ice in the river's quickwater stretches was breaking up, and I occasionally spotted steelhead leaping like silver
lightning over the ledges and rocks.

Late one day at the top of the river's chasm I found a dry log
where the sun had cleared away the snow. I sat down and stared
at the mauve-and-mandarin sky; on a distant hill the setting sun
tottered like a trembling, red sphere. I looked out across miles of

still forests and unvisited valleys. Silence pressed in on me from every side. This was the language of solitude, and I was learning to listen.

*   *   *

Meals at the cabin were adventures in ingenuity. When the cabin's supply of coffee ran out, I found a tin of rye kernels among the cupboards. These I roasted on top of the wood-stove, then crushed the charred grain for use as coffee grounds. I fashioned a smokehouse of birch bark wrapped around a frame of aspen saplings, using alder brush for fuel. In it, I smoked suckers, trout, and an occasional haunch from a rabbit. For fresh greens I kicked away the snow and gathered wintercress. I collected the dried, red berries of sumac and made borscht. I dug up Canada ginger, boiled the roots in sugar and water, and ate it like candy.

Most mornings I awoke while dawn was only a hint of pink streamers in the eastern sky. I'd have my breakfast of wild rice porridge, rye coffee, and smoked trout, and then I'd gather the tools and start on the cabin's repairs.

The work on the cabin was easy. It was pleasant to be out-doors, working with my hands and simple tools, and feeling that I was accomplishing something worthwhile. Once, in trying to level the posts that supported the porch, I needed a line level and discovered there wasn't one among the tools. Instead, I filled an empty aspirin bottle with water and found that it worked as well as any line level purchased at a store.

I hauled my drinking water in buckets from the river. My bathtub was an ancient steamer trunk that I lined with a water-proof tarp. When a snowshoe binding ripped beyond repair, I used a roll of lantern wick to make new bindings. Every day brought a challenge; every day I prevailed.

In April, deer began visiting the cabin at night. Each morning I'd find the new tracks of hares, coyotes, foxes, raccoons, and once—along the frozen river—the clear, big prints of a timber wolf. Another time I followed a bobcat trail to a hollow log and a nest of snarling, spotted cubs. Life was bursting into being all around me, but not once did I find the tracks of another man anywhere near my door.

At noon I'd sit on the porch, feasting on tea and bannock. Chickadees would land on my knees to snatch crumbs while chipmunks played at my feet, begging for handouts. The animals and I struck up an alliance to fend off the last days of winter. My part was to feed them; theirs was to make me feel that I had found a home.

Evenings were spent reading books. While I had always been a voracious reader, solitude made me ravenous for printed words. When I finished reading the books I had brought, I started in on the paperbacks and old magazines that came with the cabin. Most were so ravaged by mice that reading was impossible, but in the steamer trunk that served as my tub I found dozens of intact volumes. Many were musty outdoor books by W. Ben Hunt, E. H. Kreps, and Dan Beard. I read every one.

Most nights I fell asleep as soon as the lamps were snuffed out; other nights I'd walk through the moon shadows to a clearing where I'd roll a cigarette and watch the sky. There was always something new to see: the Northern Lights, a falling star, or the blinking lights of an airplane so distant that the sound of it was lost. At such moments I was keenly aware of being alone; yet, instead of feeling lonely, the sense of isolation and primitive solitude made me feel as if I were as much a part of the wilderness as a tree or a stone. I had come to the woods looking for answers to life, but all I found was the time to fish every day for six weeks. If I learned anything at all it was just this: solitude and being alone are vastly different things.

*   *   *

The work on the cabin was completed in late April. After that, when I wasn't fishing, I took to sitting in the sunny yard and listening to whatever was there. The advancing tide of spring was heralded by the roar of the swollen river, the cheerful trilling of thrushes, and the return of warm, southwest winds. Every twig was festooned with clear beads of snowmelt, the beads clinging for an instant before plummeting to the ground. The woods were filled with the steady, dripping patter, punctuated by the calling of geese and the drumming of ruffed grouse.

One morning I found May's first wood violet blooming in a bear's track. The discovery of the tiny flower was as delightful as receiving an unexpected letter from home. I plucked the flower, tucked it into a matchbox, and dropped it into a pocket. It was the only tangible thing I'd take to remind me of my time alone in the woods.

The next day the Jeep arrived to take me home, and though I would return to the wilderness whenever I could, it was unlikely I'd ever again have the chance to live there in solitude. I packed my things, closed the cabin, and said a silent good-bye.

Where the trail hooked sharply toward the waiting vehicle, I turned and looked at the cabin for a final time. Solitude had shown me no answers to life—only the element in which to search.

THIRTY-FOUR

Second Chances

In the North, winter is a war in which every element seems intent on crushing life. There may be beauty in the stark simplicity of a snowy landscape, but in the glitter of hoarfrost there is also doom. It lurks wherever ravens call, and in rabbit tracks that end abruptly in the snow. Winter's brief, bleak days are a chilling reminder that time is tenuous and short.

That's why steelhead season means more than the start of spring. The season starts in early April, when inland lakes are still locked beneath two feet of ice, and some streams, like the Battle River, have long stretches of frozen water.

The Battle is the one place I truly regard as my secret spot, and so I never refer to it by its real name. It starts at the foot of a waterfall, at the bottom of a gorge so narrow and deep that the sun never shines directly into the chasm. In the canyon, shelf ice doesn't rot until May. Snow can linger even longer.

Most anglers avoid the Battle. It's difficult to reach, hard to fish, and its steelhead run isn't what it used to be. But I've never visited it simply to catch trout. In its rocky, thaw-swollen spray and booming thunder, I know the meaning of indomitable.

This year, on opening day, the lake above the Battle's water-fall was icebound. Downstream, the river was frozen solid for almost a mile, so I had it all to myself. The forest trail that led down to open water was unmarked except for deer tracks. I wallowed through knee-deep snow, crawling under windfalls and climbing over rocks until, above the sound of my laboring breath, I heard the roar of quick water. Through a gap in the cedars, I caught a glint of sunlight on ice-flecked rapids. Suddenly the pall of winter was gone; in its place was excitement and action.

I went down to the river in a rush, coming out of the cedars well below the canyon. As far as I could see, the Battle was open water. It took longer than I liked for me to catch my breath, and so I lingered on a sandstone ledge, admiring a river that brimmed with reflections.

Almost a year had passed since I'd celebrated my fiftieth birthday, and for the first time in my life I felt noticeably older than I had just twelve months earlier. It wasn't the junk mail from AARP, the admission that I finally needed glasses, my first bout of gout, or the pink hint of scalp on the back of my head that hadn't been there before. It wasn't anything physical at all, but rather a sense of loss—of time squandered, trails not taken, reconciliations that would never happen, and quiet acceptance of the fact that the life you end up with is not the one you planned.

I looked out at the river, waiting for the flood of exultation-that always fills me when I visit the Battle. We were old friends. The Battle has shaped me as surely as it has shaped the canyon through which it flows. It was on the bluffs of the Battle where my young wife and I built our first home; where our son was born; where I began my career as a writer; and where so many people—who had so little—shared with me their kindness and warmth. The Battle had taught me how to live. Before that, I'd known only existence.

I no longer think about how many times I've fished the Battle. Its trees and rocks and pools and bends have weathered the years much better than I. My yesterdays now outnumber my tomorrows, and time has claimed too many friends. But in April, when the roaring Battle overflows with might, I can still believe I may live forever.

While I tied a yarn fly, a steelhead jumped, leaping over a three-foot ledge in its struggle against the current. I tossed the fly near the back eddy below the ledge. After the first hurried casts I settled down and fished deliberately. I caught a two pounder and released it, feeling as magnanimous as a king. I marched upstream, waving my rod like a banner, reclaiming what winter had tried to take from me.

The press of cold water against my legs felt familiar. So did the thrill of discovering something new at every bend. At one spot I surprised an otter. At the next pool a pair of mallards burst from the flooded bank. Under the alders the green hoods of skunk cabbage were pushing their way up through the snow. Life was changing. Its pace had quickened. Spring was on its way.

I worked my way around an oxbow near the mouth of the canyon. Here the river was jammed with ice floes. As soon as I came around the bend, the jam exploded with a black flood of ravens. I nearly fell over.

Dozens of the big, black birds rose in confusion. I could hear the rush of air through their wings. They had been swarming over a brown hump behind the ice jam. The ravens squawked madly, angry at my intrusion.

The brown hump was the carcass of a deer, which was now little more than gnawed bones and mangled hide. Ahead of me, the frozen river lay as rigid as steel as it weaved its way through the lightless canyon. The dark chasm walls throbbed with the screams of ravens.

Some people shudder at the hoot of an owl or the mournful tolling of wolves, but a friend of mine claims that the cry of a raven can turn his spit cold. Rabbits may dodge owls and deer sometimes elude wolves, but nothing escapes the ravens. Time is more relentless than talons and fangs.

I turned away from the deer and worked my way back to the sandstone ledge. There, on the north side of the river, the sun had burned away the snow. All around me were patches of warm, bare earth and the sweet, fragrant leaves of wintergreen. The air was heady with the scent of white cedar—arborvitae, the tree of life.

Fleets of white clouds filled a blue sky. I peeled off my waders and vest, bunched them up to make a pillow, and lay back to soak up the sun. I ate the apple I had stuffed in my pocket, tossed the core to a chipmunk, and closed my eyes.

I don't know how long I dozed, but when I awoke I was as languid as a bear leaving a winter den. The sun was lower, drawing warmth and color from the country. In the gathering dusk shadows raced toward the sunset. I blinked, vaguely aware of a hovering, black presence—it was a raven, sitting in a pine bough above me.

Soundlessly as a falling leaf, another raven floated down to join the first. Then, in pairs and more at a time, other ravens swooped down to roost.

It was a shock to wake up and discover ravens waiting over me. I sat up, and they bolted into the air as a flock, raving and ranting at having been robbed. For them, the easy pickings of winter were over. But only for a while. One day—too soon—winter would return.

But for now I'd found a hint of spring, the season of second chances. I gathered my gear and charged into the swirling waters of the Battle. There was a lot of river to fish before darkness fell— *miles* of river, if I'm lucky.

About the Author

Jack Kulpa lives near the lakes and streams of Wisconsin's Northwoods. An award-winning writer whose work spans four decades, he has written widely on fishing and hunting, outdoor life, and the need for wild places. A regular contributor to *Field & Stream*, he has written hundreds of articles for publications such as *Sports Afield, Outdoor Life, Fur-Fish-Game, Wisconsin Trails, Bassmaster, Conde Nast Traveler, Backpacker, Popular Lures, The Mother Earth News, Great Lakes Fisherman, Wisconsin Sportsman, Midwest Outdoors*, and *Wisconsin Outdoor Journal*. His work appears in anthologies and is often cited by the natural resources, outdoor recreation and travel industries.